Start with an Earthquake. . .

How to make presentations that wow your audience

Start with an Earthquake. . .

How to make presentations that wow your audience

Tim Stockil

Matador
9 Priory Business Park
Kibworth Beauchamp
Leicestershire LE8 0RX, UK
Tel: (+44) 116 279 2299
Fax: (+44) 116 279 2277
Email: books@troubador.co.uk
Web: www.troubador.co.uk/matador

ISBN 978 1783061 068

British Library Cataloguing in Publication Data.
A catalogue record for this book is available from the British Library.

Typeset by Troubador Publishing Ltd, Leicester, UK

Matador is an imprint of Troubador Publishing Ltd

Printed and bound in the UK by TJ International, Padstow, Cornwall

This book is for Eileen, Leo and Luke, with love.

'We want a story that starts out with an earthquake and builds up to a climax.'

Sam Goldwyn

Sam Goldwyn was one of the great producers in the glory days of Hollywood. His many films included *Wuthering Heights, The Best Years of Our Lives,* and *Porgy and Bess.* He is famous now for having made many ridiculous remarks such as *'I don't think anyone should write his autobiography until after he's dead',* but when it came to film-making, Sam Goldwyn knew what he was talking about. And his view on making films applies just as much to making presentations.

Contents

About the Author

Tim Stockil read French at Corpus Christi College, Oxford, then trained as a director at the Bristol Old Vic Theatre School. He spent ten years working in the theatre before moving into the world of training and development. He now runs his own training and development consultancy, Ci: Creative intelligence Ltd, which specialises in running 'soft skills' courses, particularly on Personal Impact, Presentation Skills, Influencing, Negotiation and many other aspects of interpersonal effectiveness. He believes that being a theatre director and being a trainer require the same skills – namely helping to draw out the best performance possible, whether from an actor or a course participant.

Tim is a Fellow of the Royal Society of Arts and is a director of the internationally renowned theatre company Cheek by Jowl.

Acknowledgements

This book could not have been written without the input and advice of a large number of people from whom I have learned over the years. Most of the content of this book has come about through actually coaching people one-to-one and delivering courses on presentation skills, and my esteemed co-trainers have been instrumental in devising exercises, developing theories and debating ideas on presenting brilliantly. In particular, I would like to thank Saul Cambridge, Lin Sagovsky, Philippa Tipper and Anna Tolputt who together form the core of my company, Ci: Creative intelligence.

The other major influence on this book has been my friend and colleague, Liggy Webb of The Learning Architect, who undertook to hold my hand (metaphorically, of course) as I wrote and without whom it would almost certainly have got halfway and stopped. Liggy, I owe you a huge debt of gratitude – thank you.

Introduction

Many moons ago, in the early days of my career, I was asked to give a speech at an IBM conference. The audience was made up not of IBM-ers, but of senior charity managers, all of whom had benefited from participating in a brilliant five-day leadership course run by IBM as part of its Corporate Social Responsibility programme. I was a (not so senior) manager of a charity at the time and had been lucky enough to have been invited to attend the course. Some months later, I was the one who was asked to speak at the conference. My task? To sum up, in twenty-odd minutes, what the course had been like and why it was so good.

I was terrible.

Somehow, the idea of telling a hundred top charity managers about a course they had all attended filled me with dread. I couldn't imagine what to say. I kept thinking that whatever I had got out of the course, other people would have got something different, and I couldn't find the right tone for the speech. In the end, I got myself so churned up about it that I abandoned my usual practice of winging it, and actually wrote out a presentation of sorts the night before, hoping it would pass muster.

It didn't pass any kind of muster. The speech was as terrible as my delivery of it.

When I sat down after delivering my pathetic presentation, sweating profusely, I could feel a hundred pairs of sympathetic eyes on me, and I knew I had failed dismally. And the worst thing was that I was normally a very confident speaker. People had told me I was engaging, funny and thought-provoking. I knew that was why I had been asked to speak at the conference, and I knew I had let my IBM hosts down badly.

If only I had known then what I know now about making great speeches. This book brings together my subsequent twenty-five years of experience in speaking at conferences and teaching presentation skills. If I had known then what I know now, I could have captivated my audience from the start and wowed them. My hope is that you will learn from my experience so that you too can captivate your audiences and wow them.

1. The Essences of Powerful Presentations

What's in this Chapter?

- * What makes an impact when you are talking to people?
- * Physical impact
- * Vocal impact
- * Emotional impact
- * The impact of language.

Speaking well in public is a skill. Like any skill, it must be learnt, even if you have a natural aptitude for it. And as with any skill to be learnt, it helps enormously if you understand the fundamental principles that underpin it.

So let's start with some fundamentals.

Whenever you talk to other people, the people listening tend to pay attention to particular elements of your communication style. Very often, people don't realise what these key elements are, assuming that the listeners are concentrating on the content of what is being said – the words, that is. And very often they are. But they are also paying attention to other aspects of what you say and, notably, how you say it. This chapter is all about identifying those key essences of powerful communication. At this stage, I only dip into some of those elements as I explore them in much greater depth later in the book.

Some Like it Yacht

When I run Personal Impact or Presentation Skills courses, I often put participants through an exercise I call, rather fancifully, 'Some Like it Yacht'. It is so called because the first time I ran it, someone told a story about working in a ship's chandlery, which was called 'Some Like it Yacht'. I thought that was rather funny so the name has stuck.

The exercise involves getting six or so participants into a circle and asking them to think of something they would like to talk about. It might be a hobby, or a sport they play; it might be about a place they visited on holiday or a special experience they had; it might be about their children, their pets or their car. It doesn't really matter provided it is something they feel enthusiastic about.

I then explain that they are only going to be asked to talk about this topic for a minute – which is not very long – and I give them a few moments to think about what they want to say to engage their audience, given that they only have a minute in which to do so.

I then drop a bit of a bombshell. I tell them that the exercise is slightly more complex than that. I explain that I am going to ask for a volunteer to start talking on a topic of my choosing. After they have spoken for a minute on hairbrushes, perhaps, or dustbin lids, I will say '*on to your own subject*'. After the first person has spoken for a second minute, I choose someone else to carry on. The second person has to talk about the first person's subject for a minute before moving on to their own – and so on, until everyone has spoken for two minutes, half the time on a topic they may or may not know anything about, and the rest of the time on their own topic, which they know well.

So someone may find themselves talking about, for example, skiing in the Dolomites without ever having skied and without even knowing where the Dolomites are. The point of this is to highlight any differences between how people come across when they know their subject as opposed to when they don't. Of course, sometimes people get lucky – perhaps they have been skiing in the Dolomites every year since they were five. If they haven't, the aim is not to repeat what the previous person said, rather to put their own spin on the subject. And if anyone starts to falter and say things like '*I can't think what to say – isn't my minute up?*', I mercilessly add time on.

3

The Point of the Exercise

Throughout the exercise, I say I want everyone to be listening to the person speaking and to be making a mental note of all the things that are having an impact on them, because at the end of the exercise I am going to record what those things are – the Essences of Powerful Presentations.

The Essences of Powerful Presentations

At the end of the exercise, we gather round the flipchart, and I ask people what factors made an impact on them. This is the sort of thing I commonly hear (in fact, this is the list from a recent course):

- * Enthusiasm
- * Passion
- * Energy
- * Eye contact
- * Smiling
- * Vocal variety – changes of tone, pitch, emphasis, volume, etc.
- * Flow, rhythm
- * Pace – changing pace to avoid monotony
- * Pauses – letting your audience digest what you've said
- * Animation – facial expression

4

* Gesture – letting your body mirror what you are saying
* <u>STORY</u>
* Making it personal – to your life and to that of the listeners
* Asking questions to involve your audience
* Making connections, referring back to what others have said
* Confidence – looking and sounding authoritative
* Humour
* Emotion
* Painting the picture, setting the scene
* Rich, descriptive language
* Metaphor, simile
* Contrast
* Reiteration and repetition
* The Rule of Three.

The Importance of Stories

You might wonder why <u>STORY</u> is set in capitals and underlined. I often have to prompt participants to come up with the word 'story' itself, although quite a few people will have inevitably told stories about their experiences. Telling stories is so much a part of being human that we tend not to notice that this is what we do, and have done since the time we started to communicate. We go home at the end of the day and tell our partners *'You've no idea what my manager said to me today. . .'* Or we meet our mates in the pub, and before long we are swapping stories – *'The weirdest thing happened to me the other day. . .'* *'Well, if you think that's weird, you should hear what happened to me in Scunthorpe,'* says someone else, and before you know it, everyone is vying to tell their story. We **love** stories. And so important are stories to making great presentations that I am going to discuss them in more depth in a separate chapter.

Facts that are Interesting and Facts that are Not

Now look back for a moment at our initial list of the things that made an impact, and think of the things that are **not** there. Very rarely does anyone say 'facts'. If they do, and I probe a bit, it turns out that facts *per se* are not interesting, though quirky or staggering or unusual facts can be – the telling detail, if you like. So, for example, being told that the population of San Marino amounts to 32,000 is not interesting; being told that when San Marino plays England at Wembley, you could fit the whole population into the arena twice over and still have room for more is much more interesting. That the American playwright, Tennessee Williams died in 1983 is not particularly interesting. The fact that he choked to death on a bottle cap is. That Henry Royce was one of the co-founders of Rolls Royce is a fact – that his last words actually **were** *'I wish I had spent more time in the office'* is an interesting fact.

Once, when I ran this exercise, a participant spent his minute reeling off a whole series of facts about his football team – Aston Villa, I think it was. By the time I got to the bottom of the second sheet of flipchart paper about twenty minutes later, I challenged the group to come up with as many facts that they had been told about Aston Villa as they could remember. No one could remember any. Not one.

And yet, most of the presentations made in businesses today are a succession of facts. Facts that the vast majority of the audience will never remember. Facts that are not quirky or intriguing or unusual. Just facts. Often they are numbers. *'Our turnover has increased by X per cent. . .' 'Seventy-two per cent of our customers say. . .', 'The firm was founded in 1989'.* Dull. Boring. Mind-numbing. Incidentally, if you do have to use numbers in a presentation, remember that even highly numerate people often find it difficult to absorb them, so always try to repeat them or re-state them in a slightly different way: *'The overall annual spend by British businesses on training is estimated to be thirty-nine billion pounds – yes, nearly forty billion pounds – which sounds a lot but actually only equates to about a thousand pounds for every worker in the country.'*

And the interesting fact is that hardly ever do our participants mention facts. They know in their hearts that facts are usually not interesting. Instead they come up with a whole list of things that really did make an impact on them.

Let's explore what they did come up with.

Energy, Passion and Enthusiasm

Enthusiasm sells, and when you are presenting, you are selling – selling yourself, your ideas, your proposals. The biggest fault I find in the people I work with is a lack of energy. I sometimes ask participants: *'If you had to put yourself on a scale from one to ten for energy, where would you be?'* The usual answer is four. So I urge them to aim for eight. Sometimes they feel that is too high, though I ask them to try it, even if it feels 'over the top'. In fact, I often urge participants to try going completely over the top, just for the experience. So they do; and I then turn to the other participants and ask if it was too much. Invariably they say no, it was just right – energetic, enthusiastic, passionate, though not too much. What seems over the top to you is almost certainly just right for the audience. So up your energy levels – it makes a huge difference.

Letting Your Body Tell the Story

Many participants on my courses complain that they don't know what to do with their hands – extraordinary, really, when you think that they have been at the end of their arms all their lives. Nevertheless, having to stand up to make a presentation seems to make many people very conscious of their hands. In my experience, you can easily get round this problem by increasing the energy you put into your presentation. If you raise your energy level, you will forget your self-consciousness and find that your hands start to make expressive gestures – they come alive, if you like. I call it 'letting your body tell the story'.

Sometimes, participants will become more animated by increasing their energy and then find that they repeat the same gesture, regardless of what they are saying. Of course, meaningless, repetitive gestures do not help. Think of Tony Blair and his open, two-handed chopping gesture which he repeated *ad nauseam*, regardless of his subject matter.

If this happens to you, you will need to think more consciously of the right gesture for the phrase or sentence, and then rehearse it. Is it a clap or a wave or a waggle of the hand? Should you point, or mime what you are saying or enumerate a list on your fingers?

Imagine a fisherman, arms outstretched, describing his latest catch – '*It was **this** big!*'; picture how someone might describe something infinitesimally small by holding their thumb and forefinger close together; think how you might describe a glass-flat sea with a horizontal gesture of your hand. Done correctly, using gesture in a presentation is an invaluable aid to making your speech come alive.

Vocal Variety and Avoiding Monotony

One of the essences of powerful communication that course participants usually want to add to the list is 'not being monotonous'. I may have to push them a bit further to say exactly what they mean by that and, almost always, they reply that it has to do with emphasis and tone of voice. Emphasis and tone depend upon energy. The more energy you put into your presentations, the more you will automatically stress certain words, vary your tone and pitch, and even your volume and pace. You will sound interesting. This is crucially important if you want people to listen to what you are saying, of course, but it also means that you imbue your words with meaning, with emotion and passion. If you say *'it is vitally important that we stay ahead of the competition'* in a monotone, it will have absolutely no impact. Put real stress on the word 'vitally' and say it with energy, and you may make your point.

Many people are not naturally endowed with interesting voices and they may have to work hard to achieve the vocal impact they want. There are some regional accents that can sound particularly monotonous, and if you have one of those, you may need to make a real effort to put some life into your voice.

Bedtime Stories

I often ask such people if they have ever had the opportunity to read a bedtime story to a young child, or if they can remember being read to when they were young. Many of the people I work with are parents, so this often rings bells with them.

At this point, I usually pull out my dog-eared copies of two children's classics – Anni Axworthy's *Along Came Toto*, and *We're Going on a Bear Hunt* by Michael Rosen – and get them to read the stories as though they were reading to a child. The change is dramatic. Suddenly, they start to give the text the energy and passion it needs. Words are stressed, whispered, growled; the pace picks up and slows down, they throw in pauses for effect, and the excitement and energy are palpable. When they apply the same magic to their own presentation, the words start to come to life. Speakers who are 'low-energy' by default often wonder if they are going over the top in delivering their speeches like this, but I have never come across anyone from the business world who has added too much vocal variety.

Pauses

One of the other typical behaviours I encounter is the inability to pause. Once many speakers get going, it seems they feel a need not to stop, so sentences roll into each other with no discernable full stops, no change of tone or volume, and no way of knowing whether the speaker has moved on to another part of their speech. In speakers who are fairly energetic in their delivery, this tends to end up sounding like gabble; if the speaker is monotonous, it sounds like a droning buzz. Both are ineffective.

The pauses matter. It is in the pause that the audience digests and absorbs what has been said, then sits in anticipation for what is to follow. Sometimes, of course, a speaker may come to a grinding halt because they have forgotten what to say next. Such a pause might seem as though it lasts forever for you, the speaker, but nearly always an audience is perfectly happy to take a pause and assimilate what you have said so far. It only goes wrong if you make it clear that you have lost your place and that you are flustered. If you do forget what comes next, one of the best things you can do is say so: *'I am having a mental blank here and can't remember what I wanted to say next. Hang on half a moment while I just look at my notes.'* If you do this with confidence, the audience will empathise, and will be completely relaxed whilst you check your notes.

The pauses often add meaning. There is a lovely poem called *Fire* by Judy Brown[1] which opens:

'What makes a fire burn
is space between the logs,
a breathing space.'

This seems to me to sum up exactly how words often take their meaning from the spaces that surround them. It also reminds us that part of the point of pausing is to breathe. The gabblers and the drones usually run out of breath – and not breathing during a speech is not a good idea. (Actually, it's not a good idea at any time!) Your breath is your 'inspiration' – which means, literally, a 'breathing in' – and, crucially, it supports your voice. I discuss both of these points in more detail in Chapter 7, 'Preparing for a Presentation'.

The Stages of a Journey

As a speaker, you are familiar with the journey you are taking your audience on, but they are not. You want to get from A to B, and hopefully you will go via H, P and Z to make it interesting, and you need to signpost those different stages of the journey. Each of those stages in your journey is a section that needs to be distinguished from the next section. I often call them 'Units of Thought' – here

---

[1] 'Fire' by Judy Brown in Loudness (Seren, 2011 www.serenbooks.com)

is one thought, and now I've just finished with that one and, listen, I am starting on the next one. Those transitions from thought to thought, from section to section, must be marked by a change of tone and a pause. Try it for yourself. Pick up a novel and read the last few sentences of one chapter and then the first few sentences of the next chapter. You will almost certainly find that the new chapter needs a new tone, a different emphasis, a distinctive voice. Break up your presentation in the same way.

Eye Contact is Crucial

There are a number of items on the list of 'Essences of Powerful Presentations' which relate to connection with the audience. Chief among these is eye contact. Far too many presenters look at the ground or at the wall or even the ceiling instead of at their audience. Everyone in the room needs to feel that you are speaking to them personally, and that your message is relevant to them and important for them. Making eye contact is the key way of doing this.

Obviously, if you are addressing a conference of three hundred delegates, you can't possibly look everyone in the eye. However, you must make sure that you look at every part of the audience. Some expert speakers consider it useful to let your eyes follow an 'M' shape followed by a 'W' shape to ensure that you connect with the whole room. This can be a useful reminder, though it shouldn't be a mechanical process. You can't just let your eyes zoom around without stopping to make definite eye contact with at least some people. Don't get stuck on looking at one person for too long, rather make sure you pause and make eye contact with a number of them. It is amazing how, as an audience member, you can feel directly connected to the speaker even if he or she has only paused to make eye contact with someone a few seats away, and not with you personally.

In fact, eye contact has another crucial role to play. There should be an energy beam that fizzes between presenter and audience, and to a large extent, that energy beam is carried by eye contact. The late, great Rudi Shelly, who taught acting at the Bristol Old Vic Theatre School, used to berate students who allowed their eyes to drop. *'On the stage in front of you,'* he would say, *'there is a big sign which says "DON'T LOOK HERE!"'*

At the risk of labouring the point, eye contact is one of the key ways in which your energy as presenter or performer touches the audience; if you are looking at the floor or out of the window, that's where your energy will go.

Facial Expression and Smiling

Facial expression is equally important as a way of connecting with your audience. As humans, we constantly read each other's faces, so you can make a huge difference to the impact of your speech by showing in your face how you feel about what you are saying. Looking at a poker face is just boring (unless you are playing poker, perhaps) but we love to watch a face that is animated. Actors spend hours exploring facial expressions, knowing that the raise of an eyebrow here or a slight twitch of the lip there can make a huge difference to their performance. Certainly, keeping a poker face (and using a monotonous vocal delivery) makes it difficult for an audience to grasp exactly what you mean. Perhaps you want to be sarcastic about something; if you don't give the audience vocal and facial clues that that is what you are doing, they will probably take your words at face value.

Smile!

Smiling is another of the key ways in which we connect with an audience. Apparently, smiling is a completely human instinct, designed to show that we are friendly, and, like yawning, it is remarkably catching. Have you ever walked down a busy street and deliberately smiled at everyone as you passed by? I guarantee you will find that the vast majority will smile back. Of course, a few may be thinking '*Do I know this person?*' and will smile back just in case they do, but mostly people will respond to a smile with a smile of their own. Try it!

Try it when you are presenting too. Smile at your audience

and they will smile back. I am not asking you for a face-splitting grin, nor a nervous twitch of the lips. Just show them that you are happy to be there and pleased to see them. Engage with your audience. Pick out friendly faces and smile at them. Pick out **un**friendly faces and smile at them too. You don't even have to smile with your lips, since an open face or a 'smiling demeanour' will have the same effect.

Naturally, you have to choose your occasion with care. Smiling broadly as you announce that the company is going into liquidation and everyone is to lose their job is not to be recommended. You may get lynched.

You are Giving Your Audience a Present

I often say to participants on my courses that they should think of a presentation as a 'present' – they are giving a 'present' to their audience. (I often talk about the importance of 'being present' too, though I pick that up later.) The point is that it is about **them,** the audience, not about **you,** the presenter. When you buy your partner a present, you don't (unless you are particularly selfish) buy them what **you** want, but rather what **they** want or need. Often, when someone is asked to put together a presentation, their reaction is to think '*What do I want to say?*' It is so much more important to think '*What does my audience want or need to hear?*'. You are giving them a present. Again, I pick this point up in more detail later in the book.

Make it Personal

There are a couple of other elements in our list above which also relate to how you connect with an audience, and making things personal is one of them. If you recount a story that has happened to you, not only are you likely to sound fluent and authoritative, you will almost certainly make the audience think *'Something like that happened to me too.'* It becomes relevant, and being relevant to your audience is crucial. Otherwise why would they want to listen?

Using lines such as *'I'm sure you've all had something of the same experience'* or *'This affects every single one of us'* helps you to connect with your audience directly. Asking questions of your audience can achieve the same end too, though you need to be clear whether you are expecting an answer or not, and if you are, you need to be prepared for whatever answers you get. (There is a whole section later on dealing with questions at the end of a presentation.) And, finally, referring back to what another speaker or someone in the audience has said earlier can be an effective way of making that all-important connection. It indicates that you have all shared a common experience, and that you have taken note of what other people have said.

Stay Calm, Look Confident

All the best speakers sound confident and relaxed, though

18

it may not be so easy if you have butterflies in your stomach and a tension headache. Nevertheless, looking and sounding confident is so crucial to great presentations that I am dedicating a whole section to this later in this book. If that's your main concern, turn to Chapter 7 'Preparing for a Presentation' now!

Emotion is Vital

I've already mentioned passion and enthusiasm. Course participants also usually mention the word 'emotion' as one of the things that had an impact on them. Emotion is often linked to humour (not jokes, by the way, just remarks that make you smile, chuckle or possibly even laugh), though when I probe further, it can reveal itself in two other ways: one, that the speaker showed some emotion whilst talking, which was in itself powerful; and two, that what has been said elicited a multitude of feelings.

If someone is giving a presentation on animal cruelty, for example, and does so without any emotional input of their own, it will probably be a very dull presentation. If the speaker is clearly moved by the plight of mistreated animals and you can hear the catch in their voice and see a tear in their eye, then some of that emotion will rub off on you. **That** is very powerful.

If someone tells you about their holiday in the Middle East and recounts how their taxi driver drove them off the road because they were being pursued by a car that he thought might ambush them (this is a story which someone recounted recently on a course), you as the audience might feel a whole raft of emotions – shock and fear, admiration at the coolness of the taxi driver or perhaps suspicion at his motives, relief that the speaker has escaped unharmed, and so on. Again, these emotions are hugely powerful elements in any good presentation.

They May Not Remember What You Said. . .

A mantra of mine is that '*They may not remember what you said, though they will always remember how you made them feel*.' I always used to think that I had invented this line but I see from the Internet that it has been attributed to many another person, famous and not-so-famous. However, I shall still appropriate it for my own ends!

This edict is particularly true of humorous speakers, of course. People remember how witty or clever or amusing a speaker was without necessarily remembering what the funny lines were. Equally, they remember boring speakers. They remember the tedium but not the content. Actually, remembering how you made the audience feel applies to any sort of presentation.

Though They will Always Remember
How You Made Them Feel

If I press my course participants to say what the purpose of most of their presentations is, very often I am told that the purpose is 'to pass on information.' However, a presentation must never just be about passing on information. There must **always** be an emotional objective as well.

You may have been tasked with explaining some unfathomable new legislation on inheritance tax, for example, and it is easy to assume that all you have been asked to do is tell people the facts about this new law. That alone would make for a dull presentation. Instead, think about what you want your audience to feel about this new legislation. Do you want them to be intrigued, alarmed, concerned? Or perhaps you want them to feel reassured that with the right advice they can circumvent this law. Or perhaps you want to rouse them into a frenzy that will lead to a popular uprising and a change in the law. That might seem like a huge step, though it is exactly what Martin Luther King did with his *'I have a Dream. . .'* speech. In a lesser way, that is exactly what a good announcer will do at a sporting event: whip the crowd up into a state of excitement. He or she will usually use an upward inflection and a crescendo as the home team comes out: *'Let's hear it for the London Wasps!'* and the home crowd will cheer and clap and whistle their approval. That is what happened at the London Olympics and Paralympics, indeed it is what happens at any big sporting event. Emotions are powerful, so always make sure you have decided how you want your audience to **feel**, and then aim for that impact. I pick up this point in much more detail in Chapter 3 'Building a Presentation'.

Using Language to Paint a Picture

Painting a picture and using rich and descriptive language come next in our list of the Essences of Powerful Presentations. There are some people who think aurally, or emotionally, though the vast majority of us think in pictures. If I am asked to think of something, I don't see words scrolling down a page, I see images – I am using my 'image-ination', as it were. So when you present, try to get your audience to **see** what you are saying by painting the picture for them. One technique to achieve this is to use rich and descriptive language. If your subject matter is very dry or abstract, you may need to think hard about how to do this. Perhaps a metaphor or simile will help. Or a story. Again, these are such fundamental aspects of great presenting that I am devoting Chapter 5 to 'Language in Brilliant Speeches'.

Rhetoric Rules, Okay?

The final few on our list – contrasts, repetition and

reiteration, and the 'Rule of Three' – are really rhetorical devices. Like many rhetorical devices, they are easy to apply and remarkably effective. I have already mentioned Martin Luther King's *'I have a dream. . .'* speech, and I could add Winston Churchill's wartime defiance: *'We shall fight on the beaches. We shall fight on the landing grounds. We shall fight in the fields and in the streets. . .'* This repetition of a key phrase – technically called anaphora – is a very impressive device, and anyone can do it.

The Rule of Three is about our liking for the rhythm and structure of saying things – examples, adjectives, anything really – in threes. In Chapter 5, I explore these and other such techniques that will help give your presentations impact.

Key Points to Remember

* **Energy** is the key to avoiding monotony, so make sure you put lots of energy into whatever you are saying.

* **Connect** with your audience – give them a 'present' that they really want or need.

* A presentation is never just about passing on information – always think about how you want your audience to **feel**.

---

2. PowerPoint or PowerPointless?

It might seem strange to have a chapter on PowerPoint[2] so early in this book. It is so prevalent in organisations, however (and not just business ones), that needs must. If you read this chapter, you will know how to use PowerPoint properly and, more importantly, you will understand why you shouldn't use it at all.

What's in this Chapter?

* Why PowerPoint is counter-productive
* Rules for using PowerPoint (if you really have to)
* For whose benefit are you using PowerPoint?
* What is more important – you or the slide?
* PowerPoint in informal situations.

PowerPoint – the Knee-Jerk Reaction

If you are a manager and you ask one of your team to prepare

---

[2] I use the term PowerPoint, which is a registered trademark of Microsoft, because it is so prevalent, though all other presentation and slide software offerings are just as counter-productive.

a presentation, you can be pretty certain that the first thing that person will do is open up PowerPoint and start to download their thoughts onto a succession of slides. In many businesses, those slides will come in the form of a template to ensure that all presentations comply with corporate branding, using specific colours, fonts and design. As a result, it is not uncommon for the staff of a company to attend an internal conference and find that all the presentations look and sound the same – and how boring is that?

For me, PowerPoint is the invention of the devil. It is rather like dynamite – it may, very occasionally, be used well and effectively though generally its impact is deeply destructive.

Why PowerPoint is Counter-Productive

In fact, for the vast majority of presentations, PowerPoint is counter-productive. Research undertaken at the University of New South Wales in 2007 demonstrated that we are able to process information effectively either in verbal or written form, though we can't do so simultaneously. Martin Waller, of *The Times*, put it like this: *'Trying to follow what someone is saying while watching the same words on the screen is the equivalent of riding a bicycle along a crowded train. It offers the appearance of making extra progress but is actually rather impractical.'* He goes on to quote Professor John Sweller who undertook the research: *'The use of the PowerPoint*

25

presentation has been a disaster. It should be ditched.'

Shakespeare and PowerPoint

When did you last go to the theatre and see the actors using PowerPoint? Can you imagine Hamlet turning his back on the audience to look at the back of the stage and intone '*To be, or not to be, that is the question*' as the words fly onto the screen? Of course not – it would be a disaster. Professional actors know that they don't need something so distracting, so disturbing, so dismissive of the audience's intelligence to deliver a fine performance. They would think any director who suggested it was completely mad. Did Winston Churchill need it? Or Martin Luther King? Or Nelson Mandela? Have you even seen David Cameron or Barack Obama or Boris Johnston using it? No, of course not. In fact, if you want to see how ridiculous such an idea is, take a look at this website: http://norvig.com/Gettysburg/. Peter Norvig, the author, imagines what the Gettysburg Address would have been like if Abraham Lincoln had used PowerPoint – classic!

The First Rule for Using PowerPoint

So the first rule of using PowerPoint in your presentations is:

Don't. Don't use it. Fight tooth and nail to abandon

26

PowerPoint, even if the culture of your company expects it. Find a different way, a more creative way, a more memorable way. Anything but PowerPoint.

How to Fight It

It is not easy to give up PowerPoint though. It may well be the prevailing culture in your organisation – you may be expected to use it, and it can be hard to fight against those expectations. Or perhaps you have been asked to speak at a conference, and you get a call from the conference organisers asking you to send your PowerPoint slides in advance so that they can include them in the conference pack. This is like being hit first with a hammer and then with a mallet. Not only is the expectation that you will use PowerPoint clear, potentially condemning you to yet another boring presentation, but also you now know that ninety-two per cent of the audience will be reading your slides from the conference pack and not listening to you at all. The other eight per cent have already read them and so have decided to skip your session altogether.

More Rules for PowerPoint at Formal Conferences

This leads us to three more rules for using PowerPoint in presentations.

Never use PowerPoint slides that have been sent to you by a colleague with instructions that you should give 'their' speech. Send them back with a terse note of thanks and create your own speech. Trying to fit your style and words into someone else's PowerPoint slides is doomed to failure.

If you really have to use PowerPoint at a conference, **never** send the slides in advance for inclusion in the delegate pack.

If you really have to provide notes for a conference audience, **insist** that they are given out **after** you have spoken.

If you have to provide notes for a conference audience, or indeed for your colleagues at work, write them up properly as notes. Your PowerPoint slides are a different medium. Giving them slides as notes is like giving someone who requested a full synopsis of a novel the Table of Contents instead. Your presentation should be dynamic, exciting, a roller-coaster of ideas and emotions; any PowerPoint slides you produce will almost certainly be dull and boring in comparison. Is that the memory you want your audience to take away?

Incidentally, many consultancy firms get this wrong, though the other way round. They write a long and detailed report and when they come to present it to the client, they put pages, often unedited, from their report onto slides. Now that is really counterproductive. Academics often do the same thing. I once attended an academic conference where nearly every speaker used slides comprising badly scanned pages of the latest section of their PhD thesis. Boring, indigestible and unreadable.

However, I am getting ahead of myself. There are some really fundamental rules that I need to establish about using PowerPoint, assuming that you really, really have to use it at all.

Use Pictures Rather than Words

Picking up on that Australian research, use words as little as possible – use pictures instead. Our brains can comfortably assimilate a visual image whilst listening to a presenter talking. We seem to be able to digest both images and speech at the same time.

Use photographs or cartoons rather than the rather poor drawings that are – or were – typical of Clipart. I once worked with someone who had to make a presentation on school arson. He had come thoroughly prepared with thirty-four slides for his thirty-minute presentation, full of facts and figures. (Not the worst I've come across, by the way – I once met a man who had prepared ninety-four slides for a thirty-minute presentation!) We managed to throw out thirty-three of the slides and we were left with just one, which was a photograph showing small groups of people watching the emergency services fighting a fire at a school.

The photograph stayed on the screen behind him throughout his talk, which concentrated on the impact of the school fire on those onlookers. One had just been appointed captain of the cricket team, although he would never get to lead his team out at home because the temporary classrooms were going to have to go somewhere, and that somewhere was the sports field. Another ran the Brownies, now sadly realising that her pack would have nowhere to meet since the school hall had burnt down. And a third was a school governor, silently weeping, devastated to see the destruction of her lovely school. The presenter revealed more about the impact of school arson by telling the stories of the people in that photograph than he ever would have by quoting all the facts in the world.

The best users of PowerPoint nearly always use pictures, and use them cleverly. I remember one speaker talking about how his feelings of being 'different' had been a feature of his childhood – and up jumped a slide of a school photo with an arrow pointing to him, the only white face in the entire picture. Another presenter used a stop-frame video to show an office block slowly being built. And a third used a line drawing, to which new elements were slowly added as she talked about her life, until it became a complete portrait of her. All of them very clever and very effective. So PowerPoint can sometimes work but it is rare. And it really does work better with pictures.

Graphs and Pie Charts Can Work

It follows that graphs and pie charts are permitted, but only if they are simple and understandable. Make sure it is clear what each axis refers to and concentrate on the central message. Don't try to put too much into one graph. If sales fell last year after three years of steady growth, illustrate this with four bars representing the growth and the fall. Don't add that homeware sales rose this year after falling last year, whereas ladieswear took a nosedive after two years of growth and menswear stayed stable. It all gets too complicated in one graph. I'm even prepared to admit that in such circumstances, it might work better to use more slides, each showing the departmental changes clearly.

A senior manager was recently introducing a course which I was running for his business. He had prepared a few slides to accompany his introduction, one of which was a nine-box matrix. Into each box he had squeezed two or three pieces of text. He showed the slide and instantly said 'You probably can't read this', and he was right, we couldn't. Why on earth, I said to him later, did you put up a slide that we couldn't read? What was the point? The pity is

31

that the nine-box matrix was potentially very interesting. If only he had scrubbed the words and just explained what each box represented.

Be More Dynamic

Incidentally, if you think you need to put up a slide of a pie- or bar chart, think instead about drawing it yourself on a flipchart. It is much more dynamic and immediate, the audience will enjoy wondering what you are drawing (that sense of anticipation is magic!), and you can easily sketch something basic and add to it as you explain what you are drawing. It doesn't matter if you are not a good draughtsman – just make a comment about the quality of the thought being more important than the quality of the drawing.

Or use props – something I shall discuss in a later chapter.

If You Must Use Words. . .

If you can't find a useful photo or cartoon, and you feel you really have to use words, then you are only allowed three or four simple bullet points per slide – five is the maximum. You really don't need any more as they represent paragraph headings, not your whole text.

Who is the Slide For – You or the Audience?

BUT – do ask yourself two key questions. One: is this slide **really** necessary? If it isn't, don't use it. And two: is this slide adding anything for the audience, or is it a crutch for you? If it is for your benefit, for example, as a reminder of your next key points, don't use it. Only use it if you are certain that it is of benefit for the audience. It is perfectly possible to have a slide on your laptop that does not appear on the screen that the audience sees if that's how you prefer to give yourself prompts.

Incidentally, there are two golden rules if you are going to list four or five bullet points on a slide. First, don't just read them out verbatim. Add a few words about each one. And second, if they are written down in a particular order, don't deal with them in a different order or miss any out. If, when you are rehearsing your presentation, you find you want to address these points in a different order, or miss one out, change the slide accordingly.

Incidentally, never flick through the slides to find one that you have already started talking about and then flick back again. This just shows that you have not rehearsed properly and that you have written your slides in the wrong order.

All this leads neatly to some more golden rules for using PowerPoint.

Why Have You Turned Your Back on the Audience?

Look at the audience and not at the slides on the screen. This is a remarkably common error that most speakers make. Remember what I said in Chapter 1 about the energy beam that connects you, the speaker, and them, the audience? That connection gets broken if you look at the screen, so keep your focus and your eye contact on the audience. If you need to check which slide is on the screen, take a quick glance at your laptop, which should be in front of you. I assume, here, that you have already checked that the projector is showing the slides on the screen properly, so you don't need to look at the screen to refer to it yourself. The slides are not there for you, they must always be there for the audience's benefit.

The Fate of the Tattooed Speaker

Make sure that the slide is not projecting onto your body. How on earth are the audience going to be able to read it if it is? At some conferences, you may find that your slides are back-projected onto the screen, so this problem shouldn't arise; though do try to ensure that the next speaker is not crossing the backstage area and letting his shadow fall across your screen. Or worse, that he has decided to explore the conference organiser's knicker elastic while their shadows give the game away – to the delight, admittedly, of the audience but the ruination, at least temporarily, of your speech. Scoff not – I have seen it happen.

Incidentally, if you have obeyed my advice not to look at the screen, you may not be aware that the knicker elastic-snapping is happening at first; however, if you are paying attention to the reaction of the audience, which you absolutely must be, you will quickly be aware that something is amiss. Then you **are** allowed to look and see what everyone else is seeing on the screen; and as you will of course be feeling confident about your material and comfortable with the way your presentation has been going, you will not get thrown by this unexpected event any more than you would be thrown by all the lights going out or the fire alarm going off or someone fainting. I shall pick up the theme of dealing with the unexpected later.

Are You in the Dark?

Make sure the audience can see you. Some conference organisers think that slides are the most important thing (these are the people who insist that you submit your slides in advance), so they dim the stage lights to a Stygian gloom to ensure that the slides stand out. Do not let them get away with this. Remember, **you** are much more interesting than any slide that has ever been created. The audience has come to witness **your** presentation, and your presentation does not just depend on hearing your words, but on seeing you too. As we learnt in Chapter 1, your gestures, your facial expressions and your animation are crucially powerful items in your presenting kitbag, and they will all be lost if you are in the dark. Otherwise, you might as well have phoned in your presentation.

This is particularly important if the conference organisers have provided a spot-lit lectern that you feel obliged to stay behind, hiding most of your body from the audience. Your body is a crucial part of your communications toolkit, so make sure you can move from behind the lectern and that you are lit if you do so. It's a good idea to use a remote control to move your slides on so that you don't have to go back to the lectern.

A No-Fly Zone

Jazzing up your slides so that they fly in from left, right and centre is not going to make PowerPoint interesting. The designers at PowerPoint added those features because PowerPoint is so inherently boring, and the flying and zooming merely makes it ever so slightly less boring – though less boring is still boring.

The Problem of the Corporate Set of Slides

Some organisations have invested money in paying a design company to create a set of slides intended, for example, for use by the entire sales force. Sometimes these are well done; they look good and they may avoid some of the common pitfalls I have been describing here.

However, they are inflexible, almost without exception. I was coaching one young executive who was obliged to use the company slides for a presentation that he was soon to make to a prospective client. Halfway through the session, we realised that two of the slides referred to products that were completely irrelevant to the prospect he was due to meet. *'Let's just cut out those two slides'*, I suggested. But no, we couldn't do that because earlier on, the introductory slide referred to the irrelevant two; and later, another referred to them again. Clearly, this firm's design company liked the 'Tell 'em what you're going to tell 'em, then tell 'em, then tell 'em what you told 'em' approach. And, because of that, there was no scope for changing or omitting irrelevant slides. So beware the corporate set of slides.

Last, but not least, why put up a final slide that just says 'Thank you'? What does it add to you just saying it?

Mind you, making *'Thank you'* your final words is hardly exciting, and you must aim to end with something much more interesting. But that's for the next chapter.

Don't use PowerPoint in Informal Situations

In this chapter, I've tended to concentrate on using PowerPoint in conferences or when talking to a large group in a relatively formal setting, because that was what it was intended for. Nowadays, people often use it in informal meetings with an audience of three or four. Don't do it! Talk to them, communicate, get a dialogue going, use a flipchart, bring a sample in, use balloons or paperclips or matchsticks, use anything but PowerPoint – please! As you may have gathered by now, I am not a huge fan of it.

Key Points to Remember

* **Don't use PowerPoint**. You don't need it and there are so many other, better ways of putting your point across.

* If you **have** to use PowerPoint, **use pictures rather than words.**

* If the slides don't benefit the audience, you've got them wrong.

---

3. Building a Presentation

This chapter is all about how to put together the contents and structure of a great presentation. It's not as simple as having a beginning, a middle and an end (although they do help of course). Follow the advice here and you will devise a richer, deeper presentation than you have ever delivered before.

What's in this Chapter?

This chapter is overflowing with goodies. It covers:

*   Creating a multi-dimensional structure for a presentation
*   Using a Mind Map approach (good)
*   Using my Post-it approach (even better)
*   The difference between your topic and your objective
*   What are you selling?
*   The importance of emotional intent
*   Concentrating on what the audience needs and wants to know
*   Finding a flow

* Starting to rehearse
* Finding powerful beginnings and endings
* A simple structure for a short presentation
* Anticipating objections
* Mapping a journey for your audience to take.

Try a Non-Linear Structure

As I suggested in the last chapter, many people when tasked with creating a presentation just open PowerPoint and start downloading their thoughts straight onto slides. Quite apart from a regrettable reliance on the iniquitous and ubiquitous PowerPoint, this approach falls down for another reason. The way that PowerPoint is structured means that you have to build your presentation in a linear fashion. This may work, for example, if your speech is very short or is on something very simple, or if you know the material backwards. However, the moment that your speech incorporates some degree of complexity, a linear approach has real drawbacks. If you create your speech this way and then step back and reflect upon its structure, you will almost certainly find that you need to shift slides around or that those points there would work better in another section of your speech – and PowerPoint is not designed with that flexibility in mind.

Mind Maps Can Help

This is where mind-mappers can come into their own. Tony Buzan's Mind Map[3] model encourages you to write your topic down in the middle of a page and then from it, create radiating branches for each section of your speech with subheadings and sub-subheadings. From this you can build your presentation in a non-linear and more flexible way.

If you are a regular mind-mapper, you'll probably use this approach anyway. If you are not, I have an approach which is not dissimilar and is even more flexible.

My Approach Using Post-it[4] Notes

This is an exercise I often ask participants to do on my Presentation Skills courses:

1. Write the **TOPIC** or subject of your presentation on a large Post-it note and stick it on the centre of a Flipchart sheet.

2. Now consider your **OBJECTIVE**. What do you want to achieve from the presentation? In particular, what

---

[3] Mind Map™ is a registered trademark of the Buzan Organisation Limited 1990, www.thinkbuzan.com.
[4] Post-it™ is a registered trademark of 3M

changes do you want to achieve or inspire in the audience? How do you want them to feel? Write your objective down on a large Post-it note and stick it next to your **TOPIC** Post-it.

3. Think of your **audience and put yourself in their shoes**. On mini Post-it notes, write down all the things that the audience **WANT** or **NEED TO KNOW**, one point per Post-it note. Stick these on your Flipchart sheet. You may want to group these by having a heading and then a series of subheadings. So, for example, you may have a heading: 'Moving into the Eastern European market' and under that you might have subheadings such as 'Which countries?', 'Local partners', 'Retail outlets' and 'Marketing opportunities', each of which you need to put on a separate mini Post-it note. Each of those may also have subheadings, each of which you should put on further Post-its.

4. Check that all these headings and subheadings are things that you want to tell the audience, and that they are things that your audience actually wants or needs to know. There may be a 'disconnect' – that is, your content does not accord with the interests of your audience. Generally, the audience's wants and needs are more important. If there is a disconnect, change some of the Post-its.

5. Now **move your Post-it notes around** until you have a structure and sequence of Post-its that works for you, and

that you think will work for the audience. You may need to draw arrows onto your flipchart to connect one section with another. Sometimes a subject that seemed at first to work under one heading now looks better under another.

6. There is lots more to do, though I suggest that this is the point at which you should 'put it on its feet' – that is to say, start rehearsing out loud. Don't just say the words; imbue them with energy and passion, and try out different gestures. Follow the sequence you have mapped out. Note good phrases, structure, links, contrasts and creative ideas. You're beginning to build a presentation!

Let's explore some of these points in more detail.

You've Got Your topic – What's Your Objective?

The second point above asks you to determine what your objective is. Not establishing this in advance is one of the great failings of many presenters. *'Can you prepare a presentation on the XYZ Project for the next monthly team meeting?'* asks your boss. He or she may want you to do this simply so that everyone in the team knows about the project. However, you must have a greater ambition than merely to pass on information. This is an opportunity not to be missed.

What do you want your teammates to feel about your

project and about your presentation? What changes of approach, attitude or behaviour would you like to see as a result of your presentation? What do you want your teammates to do once they have heard you speak about your project? These questions will help you define your objective(s).

So your topic is the XYZ Project; yet your objectives might be to inspire such excitement in your teammates about the project that when you ask them for help to meet a looming deadline, they will step forward without hesitation. Or perhaps you want your teammates to see how your project is going to affect the way the team will work in future, and to be reassured that the new way of working will have many benefits. Maybe you want your teammates to go away feeling impressed that you are making such a success of this project.

Let's take another example. I was coaching a highly technical IT specialist who works for an international company that makes semiconductors. She is brilliant at what she does, which is to get feedback from customers about how they want to use the firm's products and then to tweak the products so that they meet those needs and at the same time knock spots off their competitors' products. She had come to me because she needed to give a presentation to customers about the new product she had developed following their feedback.

'So,' she said, 'my topic is the FG47596, and my objective is to tell them all about the changes I have made to the old FG47212.'

'You have the topic right', I said, 'though not the objective. How do you want them to feel about the new FG47596?'

'I want them to be impressed.'

'How impressed?'

'Very impressed.'

'Very impressed so that. . . ?'

'Very impressed so that they can see how I have incorporated their needs.'

'Okay, so you want them to be very impressed with the new product and with its capabilities, so now what do you want them to do as a result of being that impressed?'

'Well, to buy it, I suppose.'

'Exactly! So now you have your objective. You want them to be so impressed with your new product that they will instantly put in a large order. You want them to buy it.'

Selling Something and the Importance of Emotional Intent

This is nearly always the key objective behind a presentation. You, the speaker, are selling something. You are selling an idea or a product or yourself. You are selling a feeling. There must be an emotional intent behind what you say.

If you are giving a presentation about the melting of the polar ice caps, you don't want people to come away unmoved. You don't want them leaving your session saying *'Well, now I know how many square miles of ice cap are melting every year. How mildly interesting.'* You want them to come away incensed, shocked, appalled. You want them to lobby their MP immediately, make a donation to the cause, sign your petition.

You may feel that your subject matter is not as emotive as the melting of the ice caps, though you still need to find an emotional objective. Do you want them to feel intrigued, shocked, surprised? Proud, amused, concerned? Or perhaps inspired, motivated and moved? If your task is the regular quarterly financial presentation, take a view on the subject and aim for an emotional reaction, and it will transform your presentation.

In fact, this concept of 'emotional intention' should be a constant part of your presentation because it will change depending on where you are in your speech. Your overall intention may be to shock your colleagues about, let's say, the dire state of the company finances, yet you may also want to speak about how the Watford store has exceeded all expectations and posted record results. Here, perhaps, your emotional intention is to surprise the majority of the audience and to make the Watford team feel proud. Then you may move on to warn the Watford team as well as everyone else not to get too complacent or smug. Thus your emotional intention has changed again. An actor preparing a part (particularly a long soliloquy) will constantly be thinking *what effect do I want now? How do I want my audience to react at this point?*' The emotional intention can change from line to line.

I often give participants on my courses an extract from a play and get them to discuss what the emotional intention is and how it changes through the speech. Take Henry V's St Crispin's Day speech, delivered to his soldiers just before he urges them into battle:

This day is called the feast of Crispian:
He that outlives this day, and comes safe home,
Will stand a tip-toe when the day is named,
And rouse him at the name of Crispian.
He that shall live this day, and see old age,
Will yearly on the vigil feast his neighbours,
And say 'To-morrow is Saint Crispian.'
Then will he strip his sleeve and show his scars,

And say 'These wounds I had on Crispin's day.'
Old men forget: yet all shall be forgot,
But he'll remember with advantages
What feats he did that day: then shall our names,
Familiar in his mouth as household words,
Harry the king, Bedford and Exeter,
Warwick and Talbot, Salisbury and Gloucester,
Be in their flowing cups freshly remember'd.
This story shall the good man teach his son;
And Crispin Crispian shall ne'er go by,
From this day to the ending of the world,
But we in it shall be remember'd;
We few, we happy few, we band of brothers;
For he to-day that sheds his blood with me
Shall be my brother; be he ne'er so vile,
This day shall gentle his condition:
And gentlemen in England now a-bed
Shall think themselves accursed they were not here,
And hold their manhoods cheap whiles any speaks
That fought with us upon Saint Crispin's day.

King Henry might well have an overarching intention – to motivate his soldiers to fight – but there are other emotional responses he seeks in this speech. He wants them to imagine how proud and superior they will feel when they show their scars to others who weren't fighting that day; he wants them to feel as one with him, as his equal, his brother; he wants them to feel that today will mark them with immortality; and so on. And so it must

48

be for you when you are delivering a speech. You must constantly think about how you want your audience to feel at each point in the presentation as well as have an overarching emotional intention so that they go away with that feeling in their hearts.

Recall what I said before – they may not remember what you said, but they will remember how you made them feel.

What Does Your Audience Want and Need to Know?

Let's go back to our Post-it note process for creating a presentation. Points three and four are principally about the importance of setting aside what you want to say and instead thinking about what the audience needs or wants to know. Remember, you are giving the audience a 'present', and any good present is going to be something that the recipient wants or needs. Or, as Ken Haemer of AT&T said, *'Designing a presentation without an audience in mind is like writing a love letter and addressing it "to whom it may concern".'*

Of course, in many instances you may have a very clear idea of what you want to tell your audience. As a leader, you may have key information to impart, a message to give, although you still need both an emotional objective and to put yourself in your audience's shoes – what do they need to know? And what do they want to know? You may

49

have to convey a message which is unwelcome – that an office is going to close, perhaps, or that you have just lost a large account – yet you still have to think about what your audience wants to know. They may not have wanted the disagreeable central message, yet there will certainly be things they **do** want to know. If the office is closing, what impact will that have on their jobs? Can you reassure them? Will there be changes in your approach to customer retention as a result of that lost account? Can you inspire them to work harder on customer service so you don't lose any more?

A Typical Disconnect

I find that there is often a 'disconnect' between what a speaker wants to say and what an audience wants or needs to know. A common example is when an IT expert is invited to make a presentation to, let's say, human resources staff about the new software system due for installation. The IT expert may well want to go into minute detail about the technical specifications of the software, because that's what excites him (it's usually a him); however, what the HR audience really wants to know is how quickly and smoothly the new system can be installed and how easy will it be to use.

Of course, such an IT expert may be invited to give a talk to other IT experts about the new software system, in which case the audience are likely to be as excited as he is about the technical specifications. That is a different presentation. The topic may be the same, though the objective will be different and the content will be different too. The same thing would apply if you were in marketing for a bank, for example, and had prepared a presentation on a new advertising campaign that was about to hit the media. Your speech to the branch staff would be – **must** be – quite different from the one you give to the call centre staff.

I once had to sit for what seemed like hours listening to my erstwhile Chief Executive give an interminable speech at a company awayday in which he told us what the (non-executive) Chairman felt about our work. None of us cared less about the Chairman's views; what we really wanted to hear was what the Chief Executive felt. This was a classic case of our CEO concentrating on what was concerning him (after all, he was the one who kept being earbashed by the Chairman) rather than thinking about what we, the staff, wanted to hear. His speech caused a considerable degree of frustration and demotivation, which was exactly what he had **not** wanted. He needed to put himself in our shoes – what did we want and need to know?

Moving Your Post-it Notes Around

We have now arrived at point five in the Post-it exercise. This is all about checking that you have the right Post-its and moving them around to create a journey, a through line for the presentation you are creating.

It is quite common at this point for participants on my courses to start taking off some Post-its and putting new ones on. Being clear about both the objective and the focus on the audience's needs and wants can radically change the content of your speech. When you change the content, you often find that you change the order and even the whole structure of your talk.

Let's take the IT expert and the new software example I gave above. Originally, the content of the talk – what he had written on the smaller Post-its – included all sorts of technical information, mostly expressed in jargon and acronyms. Now, bearing in mind the HR staff's needs and wants, he will be talking about how the software will make the process of recording absences, holidays and illness so much easier and quicker; and he will make it clear that they will all be able to learn how to use it in a short half-day of training. It has become a different presentation.

What's the Flow? Is the Road Map Clear?

Once you start changing the content, you find that you often have to change the sequence of the talk. Does one section flow smoothly into another? Is there a link that will connect one subheading with another section?

Perhaps a section that is currently languishing in the middle of your speech should really be your climax?

This is where my Post-it note process scores over Mind Maps – it is so easy just to move a Post-it note to another place on the flip chart sheet, or take one off and replace it with four new ones. It becomes rather like a puzzle, moving pieces around until they seem to fit. You may eventually need to draw arrows on your flipchart page to show which section follows which. If you arrive at a structure that seems to work for you, you will probably find that you will be able to remember it and deliver it well.

Get Up and Try it Out

Nevertheless – and this is what comes out of point six in the exercise above – do try it out, ideally with a real live audience who are prepared to give you feedback. What works for you may not work for them. You may have to make the connections clearer. This way, you will learn more about whether your presentation works or not than you ever will by sitting down and writing your speech out. It will soon become clear whether the structure and content serve your needs and, particularly if you have a friendly colleague giving you feedback, you will soon discover whether your objective and emotional intent are clear.

Don't Write it Down

This leads me onto a major warning: unless you are a good writer with a real ability to script spoken English, don't try to write your speech down at this stage. Nearly all the business people I work with drift into corporate-speak – the sort of thing you would put in a formal report – the moment they start to write out their speech. However, a presentation is a different medium – it's not the written word, it's the spoken word. Great presenters don't sound as though they are mouthing an official report, they sound as though they are talking to their friends at dinner.

To illustrate the difference, take a look at the following sentence which comes from a report delivered by a senior sales manager: *'When it comes to our sales activity, there are certain things we persist in doing which are difficult to implement and provide us with a low return and the danger here is we spend time carrying out these actions because we perceive they add value or perhaps we enjoy doing them because they are a sort of comfort blanket or we're stubborn, but they are not important, add little or no value and waste a good deal of time.'*

Try saying the sentence out loud. I am pretty certain you will run out of breath, and the meaning may not be at all clear to a listener. If you wanted to say the same thing in a speech, you might say something like this:

'When it comes to sales, we keep on doing the things we shouldn't be doing. Sometimes those things are difficult to do, but we keep on trying. And sometimes they give us a low return on investment. Why do we do this? Do we think they add value? Are they a comfort blanket, and we enjoy the sense of familarity? Or are we just plain stubborn? Whatever the reason, we are doing the wrong things. They are not important. They add no value. They waste our time.'

I am not against writing a speech down if you have the skills to do so. Nor am I against writing it down in full, if you have a long, complex or legally binding speech to make. Just don't write it down too early. Almost always, it is more effective to try a speech out, improvising words and phrases and sentences as you go, noting the ones you like, and only afterwards trying to write down what you said. Then, there is much more chance that you will write down spoken English rather than long, elaborate sentences that are more at home in a formal report.

Most people are perfectly capable of improvising like this, provided they have done the Post-it note exercise thoroughly, because they know their subject and because they have a structure and a flow to their presentation. If you don't know your subject well, you may feel you need to write more than just bullet points. You still need to bear in mind that a speech requires spoken English and not written English, and speaking it out loud is the best possible way of finding out if it sounds natural.

The Sam Goldwyn School of Presenting

There are more things you can do to help create a structure for a presentation and there are some standard structures to try that can help a lot. I am not a great fan of the often quoted 'Tell 'em what you're going to tell 'em, tell 'em, then tell 'em what you told 'em' as it always seems to deny the audience any intelligence at all, though some people like it and for a simple speech it might work well. I feel it tends to lend itself to boring repetition (repetition doesn't have to be boring, of course), and most speakers who swear by it start their presentations with a long rigmarole which sends me to sleep straightaway.

I am more an advocate of the Sam Goldwyn school. Sam Goldwyn was a great film producer (as in Metro-*Goldwyn*-Meyer) in the golden days of Hollywood, and he was renowned for saying some pretty inane things: '*A hospital is no place to be sick*', '*If I look confused it is because I am thinking*' and even '*A bachelor's life is no life for a single man.*' However, he did say one thing that rings true – so true, in fact, that I have purloined part of it for the title of this book:

'*We want a story that starts out with an earthquake and builds up to a climax.*'

Find Your Earthquake

Sam really knew what made a good film, and the same thing applies to a good presentation. Far too many speakers start off by saying something like *'Thank you very much for inviting me today. I'm Jo Bloggs and I am Head of HR at Megacorp plc* (the audience already knows this because someone else has introduced her) *and I've been asked to come to speak to you today about the impact of the new legislation on pensions and part-time workers* (the audience already knows this too as the speech has been introduced as Jo Bloggs on the new legislation affecting pensions and part-time workers) *and I have to say that I am really pleased to be given this opportunity because I think that maybe some of you in the audience will find what I have to say quite interesting. . .'* By this time, ninety per cent of the audience have fallen asleep and the rest have started imagining how to assassinate Jo Bloggs.

So one of the key elements of developing a good presentation is to find a way of starting it that makes people sit up and take notice. Start with an earthquake. It is very rare that you need to tell people who you are. If it is an internal presentation, the audience probably knows you anyway; if it is a speech at a conference, you will probably be introduced by the conference host. And in any case, it doesn't have to be the first thing you say.

Lin Sagovksy, one of my regular co-trainers, demonstrates how to start with an earthquake by coming into a room to make a short presentation wearing a plastic bag on her head. This is not a superfluous gesture, I hasten to add, but connects to the core of her topic. I have seen all manner of speakers' entrances: coming in juggling apples; wearing a chef's toque and apron and carrying a frying pan; saying the single word *'Balls!'* (This last one was a cricketer, as it happens.) All of them made the audience sit up and take notice. It was clear from there on in, the talk was not going to be boring.

It doesn't have to be so dramatic, of course. Perhaps you can pose a really interesting question – *'What would you do if the postman ran off with your dog?'* Or tell a story – preferably about something that happened to you rather than just a story you heard once. Or perhaps you could make a bet with the audience, or draw something on a flipchart and ask them to guess what it is, or say something shocking. I was once asked to give the homily at the funeral of Daphne, the mother of my oldest friend. Daphne's late husband had been a member of the armed forces and a staunch, not to say diehard, Conservative who used to swear at the television when a Labour politican came on. You could have been forgiven for thinking that Daphne shared his views. So when I opened my address by saying *'Many of you may not be aware that Daphne was a lifelong member of the Communist Party'*, the collective gasp from the congregation could have been heard twenty miles away.

There are simply millions of ways of starting a presentation that grab the audience's attention – though *'Good afternoon, I'm Jo Bloggs. Thanks for inviting me. . .'* is not one of them.

Building to a Climax

Sam Goldwyn's maxim also refers to the end of your speech – build to a climax. Far too many presentations just dribble away to nothing, leaving the audience not sure whether the speaker has finished or not. Or the speaker says *'Thank you'* and stops talking, so the audience suddenly realises they have finished.

So make sure your presentation ends with a climax. Often the simplest climax is to repeat your key message so that the audience leaves with it ringing in their ears. Or make it clear to the audience what it is you want them to do next, as a result of what you have said. This is often something that speakers miss out, so their audience is unsure what they are expected to do. A good speaker will link this to how he or she wants the audience to feel. If you have got the audience feeling inspired or shocked or concerned, then the logical next step is that they should do something as a result. *'So if you too feel appalled at the fate of greyhounds past their racing prime, there is a simple solution – adopt one today!'*

A Simple Structure for a Short Pitch

Ending on saying what you want your audience to do next is one of the tenets of my friend and colleague, Lin. She recommends a very simple structure for a short presentation or pitch:

*   Grab the audience's attention
*   Make it relevant
*   Make your core message clear
*   Give one (or more) example(s)
*   Say what you want them to do next.

This works remarkably well for a short pitch and can be easily expanded to work for a longer presentation. The meat in the sandwich may expand – there may be a number of messages and numerous examples – though the principle of grabbing their attention (starting with an earthquake), making what you are saying relevant to the audience and ending with a climax that clearly states what you want them to do next is exemplary.

Focus on the Benefits to the Audience

One of the other things that many speakers forget is to

focus on the benefits to the audience. This partly relates to Lin's point about making it relevant, and partly to putting yourself in the audience's shoes. Think about what the audience wants and needs to know and also what objections they may have to what you are saying.

Let's say you are speaking to colleagues about a new flexitime system that the company wants to implement. This may not be relevant to everybody now, though you could paint a picture of a time when all staff would appreciate the flexibility of changing their hours of work; and at the same time, by putting yourself in your audience's shoes, you can stress how no one will be forced to change their hours overnight, that there will be plenty of time for negotiation and that the system will not be operational for three months, or whatever.

Anticipating Objections

I call this last part 'Heading them off at the pass.' Heading them off at the pass in presentation-speak is about anticipating objections to what you are saying and dealing with them in your speech. This is particularly important if you are speaking about a proposed change such as a new work process. There are bound to be some people who will be resistant to the changes you are suggesting, so when creating your presentation, ensure that you include a section which acknowledges this resistance and explains how you will minimise the impact. Otherwise, you are bound to have to deal with a whole load of awkward questions and perhaps even simmering resentment.

Do you have a *Leitmotif?*

Finally, something else to consider when you are constructing your presentation is whether there is a metaphor or an overarching idea or *leitmotif* that will connect all the sections of your speech. Does the speech as a whole have the feel of a journey, or a race, or a game, for example? Perhaps early on in your speech, you referred to the ferocity of a leopard – can you repeat the animal metaphor throughout, so you build an entire zoo? Provided this approach is not too forced, it can work really well; however, if ever you are struggling to make the connection, you probably need to abandon it. One finance director I worked with described the quarterly results by likening them to the ingredients of an omelette. In fact, he didn't just describe them as such, he actually cooked an omelette on stage as he was talking – brilliant!

Having such an overarching theme or metaphor for your speech doesn't always work, though it is always worth exploring in case one occurs to you.

Key Points to Remember

* Use a flexible, non-linear approach such as my 'Post-it notes' exercise to form the initial structure of your presentation.

* Ensure your objective goes beyond your topic, so you are not merely passing on information.

* Remember, your talk is for the benefit of the audience, so tell them what they need or want to know, not just what you want to tell them.

* Start with an earthquake and build to a climax.

4. Adding a Touch of Creativity

In the last chapter, I explored creating the content and structure of your presentation; now, I want to explore how to make your presentation creative. This chapter is all about finding ways to make a speech different, memorable and imaginative.

What's in this Chapter?

As you will have gathered by now, I am a fan of unusual, memorable presentations. Thinking beyond PowerPoint is a start, though you can go much further to give your presentations impact. There are an infinite number of ways to make your presentations creative; this chapter explores a few of them:

* Stories (including examples)
* Metaphor
* Using props
* Interacting with the audience
* Getting the audience active
* Using actors
* Using your own strengths.

The Power of Stories

First, think about stories. What stories can you tell that will illustrate your points, make them relevant or personal, or bring them to life? A story doesn't have to be long or complex. For example, when running a course on presentation skills, I stress how stories have been the way humans have communicated since we first began to speak, and I often launch into this one:

There was a caveman coming back home at the end of the day: 'Well, darlin', I was out on the prairie, hiding behind this big boulder and along comes this hairy mammoth. So I picks up this rock, see, and I chuck it – and blow me if it doesn't hit the mammoth straight between the eyes. It keels over, dead as a dodo. So that's why we've got hairy mammoth for tea – and breakfast – and lunch. . .'

It doesn't take more than a few moments to tell, yet it makes the point.

A Longer Version – now about Imagination and Invention

I was once a participant on a course myself, in which everyone was asked to come back the next morning with a story to present. I thought I would elaborate on the story above and it became a tale about invention:

The Thal family lived in a cave. It wasn't warm, but it was dry, and that was the main thing.

Nea stayed at home while her man, Anders, was out at work. Well, that was the way it was back then. Not that she had to do much – tidying away the logs, throwing out last night's bones, a bit of decoration. She was getting pretty good at sketching deer, she thought.

Anders' role was to hunt the deer and he wasn't bad at it. Every evening, he'd come back from the hunt, bringing home the bacon. Well, not exactly bacon – more likely a badger and some berries.

One night, he did not come home.

Nor did he the next day. Nea abandoned her latest chef-d'oeuvre *– Two Buffalos Galloping in the Moonlight – to look for him, but there was no sign. That evening, Nea stood at the mouth of the cave, arms folded, foot tapping, just itching to give him a piece of her mind. Still no Anders.*

It was only on the evening of the third day that a sweaty, dusty Anders came staggering up the hill to the cave.

'Where the hell have you been?' screamed Nea. 'Don't you realise some of us haven't eaten for three days? Flirting with that flame-haired floozy from down by the ford, I

shouldn't wonder! You're a very naughty boy!' Nea paused. 'Go on, then, what's your excuse? I expect you've got some story or other.'

'I have, as a matter of fact, if you'll just shut up long enough to let me tell you, you grouchy old grampus.' You'll notice that the idea of emotional intelligence had not really caught on by this time.

Nea did shut up eventually, so Anders told her his story: 'Well, you see, darling, I was down on the prairie, lurking behind this big boulder, when along comes this great hairy mammoth. So I picked up this rock and I hurled it at the mammoth – and blow me down if it didn't hit him right between the eyes. He keeled over, twitched a bit and then lay dead as a dodo – or whatever those birds were called, you don't see them around here any more.

'So there I was, on the prairie, with a dead mammoth. Now, your dead mammoth is not like a squirrel or a marmoset – you can't just toss it over your shoulder and trot off home. I mean, I could just about lift its trunk but that was about it. So what was I going to do? I thought about cutting it up and bringing you the best fillet steaks, but what a waste – this beauty would feed us through the whole winter, given a bit of salt and an icehouse.

'Then I thought, I could come back and get you to come and help. No, that would be no good – that Fred and Barney,

they'd be down there, hacking it to pieces, before I'd gone a hundred yards.

'No, I had to think! How was I to get it back here? So I thought; and I thought; and I thought.

'And then, bingo! Why not roll it here?

'So I started to chip blocks of stone into round things with holes in the middle that I could put a branch through. I made four of these round things – I was going to call them "polos" but I thought that was a silly name, so I've called them "wheels" instead – and I made a cart – that's my name for a sort of platform with wheels – and I levered – what, levered? Never mind – I levered the mammoth onto the cart and I wheeled it back here. And that's why there is hairy mammoth for tea – and breakfast – and lunch. . . . So stop standing there with your mouth open, Nea, get inside and get the fire going.'

'Fire?' shrieked Nea. 'What the hell's fire?'

Short Stories

Many stories are really short. Here's one that is just six words long:

'For sale: Baby shoes, never worn.'

How powerful is that? It is also elliptical in that it doesn't tell you a straight narrative but allows you to invent many different narratives of your own. The Japanese verse form, Haiku, now widely adopted (and adapted) by poets writing in English, typically only takes three short lines (and sometimes a set number of sounds or syllables). A Haiku often seems to be a story in miniature that succeeds because of its allusive nature – it suggests the meaning instead of spelling it out.

Gusts of wind on the hill
A red balloon floats
The dogs run round barking.

Stories for All Occasions

So a story can be short or long, and it can have many functions. It may show how a different part of the company, or another organisation altogether, experienced success or failure with the sort of issue, project or product that you are discussing. Perhaps your aim is to inspire your colleagues to action or to change something. Or perhaps you are more concerned about values, and your story demonstrates how you think people in the organisation should behave. There are stories about leadership and responsibility, about teamwork and change, about processes and transitions, about myths and legends (both ancient Greek and modern corporate) and about truth and reconciliation. There are stories about everything.

A Story as a Summary

You may wish to use a story to sum up what you have been saying. My colleague, Philippa Tipper, who is a professional storyteller as well as a trainer, often finishes a course on communication skills with this story:

There was a king who lived in a far-off land. As he was getting old, he decided that he would pass his crown to one of his children. So he called them into the Great Hall and said: 'My children, I want you to go out into the world and bring back to me the sharpest and the sweetest thing you can find. And the one who succeeds will succeed, as it were.'

The firstborn Prince leapt onto his trusty steed and galloped off to the West. After a time, he came to a forest and heard the sound of chopping. And there, in a clearing, was a woodsman with an axe, chopping down trees. The Prince could not believe how cleanly and quickly the woodsman cut down those trees with that axe – surely that must be the sharpest axe in the world. So the Prince offered the woodsman one hundred gold coins for the axe, a price that was gratefully accepted, and he rode off again. A bit later, he came across an old woman who was tending some beehives. He asked if he could taste her honey. 'Why, yes, kind Sir, it's the sweetest honey in the world.' So he tasted it and truly he had never sampled honey as sweet and luscious before. More gold coins changed hands and the Prince started on his way back to the Castle.

The younger Prince had ridden off to the East. After some time searching, he came across a market and in one of the market stalls was a woman selling pins and needles. 'Get your needles 'ere,' she shouted, 'the sharpest needles in the world, they'll go through anything.' Flourishing his purse, the Prince promptly bought a book of the magnificently sharp needles. The Prince walked on and came across another market stall where the stallholder was whipping up a pink concoction which he called Candy Floss. Intrigued, the Prince stopped to try some and was instantly convinced that here was the sweetest stuff in the world. A few moments later, he was on his way back to the castle with the needles in a pocket and a cloud of Candy Floss in his hand.

Back at the Castle, the King was waiting patiently – or perhaps impatiently – for his children to return. In came the firstborn Prince and he presented his father with the axe and the honey. The King tried out both and exclaimed: 'Truly this is extremely sweet honey. And this axe' – he split a hair with it as he spoke – 'this axe is magnificently sharp.' As he said this, the second Prince appeared, and the King hurried to try out the needle. 'Ouch! That really is sharp' – and the Candy Floss: 'My boy, this is so sweet my teeth are all falling out. But are these the sweetest and sharpest thing in the world?'

At that moment, the door of the Great Hall opened and in came the King's daughter, the Princess. In her cupped hands, she cradled a small parcel of leaves, which she presented to her father. The King carefully opened the parcel of leaves, and there, unmistakably, was a human tongue.

'Ah, my darling child,' the King said. 'A human tongue. Now there truly is the sharpest and sweetest thing in the world. For when it talks of love and desire and bonuses and promotions, it is indeed the sweetest thing; but when it talks of hate and jealousy and cuts and redundancies, it can be so easily the sharpest thing.'

So you all own the sweetest and the sharpest thing in the world – use it wisely and well.

Tell Your Own Stories

Good stories, well told, can transform your presentations, and luckily for you, there are loads of books and websites that offer you examples, often categorised under suitable headings – 'Stories about Teamwork', 'Stories about Values', etc. Unluckily for you, your audience may have seen the same books and websites, so tread carefully. It is almost certainly better for you to tell a story about something that happened to you than it is to try to recount a story such as the one about the human tongue above. It will sound more personal and authentic. If you do decide to tell a story that is not personal to you, make sure you rework it in your own words and rehearse it really thoroughly.

Metaphor – the Way We Make Sense of the World

Closely related to stories is the use of metaphor. A good metaphor can make what we say much more compelling and vivid because metaphors provide a parallel to the actual situation. That is the way in which we humans have always tried to make sense of the world. If you are presenting a new thought or a plan for change, help the audience to grasp it by showing them the parallel world through a metaphor. We use metaphors all the time, by the way, often completely unwittingly, so don't feel that this is an alien concept. Perhaps you have come in from a jog and complain that you are 'shattered'. You are probably comfortable talking about 'floating' an idea, calling someone's argument 'shaky', or describing someone's views as 'food for thought' – all everyday metaphors.

Overarching Metaphors

You may find that there is a metaphor that encompasses your whole speech. I once heard a manager give a terrific speech likening his company's performance to a hospital casualty department. The parallels were telling. He started with the negatives – the apparent chaos, the way patients (customers) were ignored, the soulless surroundings – then he moved on to the positives, such as the teamwork, the ability to see what was urgent and deal with that at the expense of the merely important, and then the end result which was often a near miracle dragged from disaster. Stephen Fry once gave a speech about the importance of the arts, describing them as the landscape of the country and how a lack of investment would lead to desolation. Again, an overarching metaphor that encompassed the whole speech.

Metaphors for Power and Impact

A metaphor can also be a short but telling way of making a point come alive. Martin Luther King's famous 'I have a dream. . .' speech is full of metaphors. One sentence goes:

'I have a dream that one day even the state of Mississippi, a desert state, sweltering with the heat of injustice and oppression, will be transformed into an oasis of freedom and justice.'

And he ends with:

'With this faith, we will be able to transform the jangling discords of our nation into a beautiful symphony of brotherhood.'

Metaphors all over the place.

So as you prepare your presentation, think about what parallels there are. You may be talking about something fairly mundane, perhaps a new system of logging holidays and sick leave, just don't let your speech be equally mundane. Perhaps there is a parallel with a school timetable, ordering from the Next Directory, or the way you book your local squash court. Use a metaphor to bring it to life.

The Overworked Metaphor

Do be careful, however, about the overused metaphor. I work a good deal with a major insurance company who used to sponsor rugby in England (which insurance company hasn't?) and as a result, presentation after presentation featured PowerPoint slides of scrums and throw-ins with often laboured parallels between the work of the company and rucks and mauls and the other jargon of rugby. Sometimes it worked, mostly it didn't.

Finding Your Metaphor

You may be thinking that this is all very well, but you can never seem to come up with an effective metaphor or parallel. You are not alone – good metaphors don't just grow on trees, ready for plucking by any passer-by. However, there are some simple ways of exploring the options. Start off by listening to your own words. Because we use metaphor all the time, we often choose one instinctively which can be expanded.

I worked with one manager who had to make a speech on internal communications. In one early session, he spoke about a rumour having gone viral, a familiar metaphor from the world of YouTube. It led us to explore communications as though they were a virus to be prevented or contained, a metaphor which worked well for part of his speech.

Alternatively, you might like to take your subject and play the old game of 'If my subject were a _____, what would it be?' You can fill in the blank with thousands of words – a vehicle, a race, an animal, a meal, a landscape, a film, a piece of music, whatever takes your fancy. Or perhaps there is a television programme or quiz that can provide you with a new and fresh metaphor for your presentation? Many metaphors will lead to nothing, some will lead somewhere yet may not hit the nail exactly on the head, and perhaps one will spark an idea that leads to a metaphor that really brings your presentation to life.

Be careful, though. Any wacky idea needs to serve the subject matter. It is no good coming up with a metaphor for your whole presentation, however great you think it is, if it leaves your audience confused.

Propping Up Your Speeches

My next suggestion for making your presentation more creative is to consider the use of props. I've already mentioned my friend Lin coming in with a plastic bag over her head; what I didn't mention was that she ended her pitch by whipping out a 'bag for life' as a contrast to the flimsy plastic bag that we so often use for a few moments and then discard. Props can help make your presentation much more memorable.

I worked with one presenter who needed to explain how the new 'No Win, No Fee' legislation differed from the previous legal aid system for dealing with, for example, claims against a local authority for unrepaired pavements. He particularly wanted to make clear what happened to any money paid out as a result of the claim. Because the conference was going to be set up with the audience sitting around tables cabaret-style, we were able to devise a speech that made good use of props – in this case some of the old style cloth moneybags that banks used to keep smaller plastic bags of coins in. The speaker allocated different roles to different tables. One table repesented the claimant, Mrs Haythornthwaite, who had tripped over a wobbly pavement slab and had broken her hip. Another table represented the local authority and the other two tables were the authority's solicitor and the claimant's solicitor. The money all started on the local authority's table, and, as the presenter narrated what happened, the bags were passed to the other tables as appropriate. By the end, it was abundantly clear that the authority had no money left, Mrs Haythornthwaite had a little, and the lion's share had found its way to the solicitors' tables. A simple and very effective use of props.

Some years ago, I worked with another couple of presenters who had to make a joint speech about how things had changed in their business over the past ten years. We used props from the decade before – toys of the time that were short-lived fads, a mobile phone that was the size of a brick and so on – to help underline how far and how fast things had changed in that time.

I've always admired the finance director who made a speech about the company results with a row of glasses and a large jug of water in front of him. As he spoke about different aspects of the results, he poured water into each of the glasses, a lot or a little depending on the amounts he was talking about. Although the glasses all looked clear, when he poured the equally clear water in, the liquid changed colour. The last glass stayed clear until he passed his hand over it at the climax of his speech and the liquid suddenly began to fizz and pop – magic! I'm not sure if he was a chemist or a magician; either way, it made for a memorable presentation.

I've already mentioned another finance director who cooked an omelette on stage, and a presenter who came on juggling (he had a good metaphor about juggling priorities too), and there are many, many more great examples of using props to bring your presentation to life. One manager who came on one of my courses used colleagues as props. He happened to be in a department with one very tall colleague and one very short one and two others of middling (though different) heights. He brought them on stage one by one, giving each of them a separate description, until they all lined up next to each other and became a living bar chart. I have seen other speakers effectively use shoes, percussion instruments, fruit and (indoor) fireworks, and I am sure there are myriad other possibilities.

There is a story, possibly apocryphal, that when the Disney board was discussing the creation of the Animal Kingdom, they had reached a state of indecision until one of the directors brought a real, live leopard to the boardroom. It was only the proximity to a wild animal that persuaded them to try to replicate for others the same sense of excitement and awe that they had felt themselves. Of course, that was not a presentation, though the impact of bringing in that prop (if we can call a live leopard a prop) was indisputable. First, find your leopard. . . .

Panel Presentations

Sometimes, you may be asked to present at a conference as part of a panel. This approach is often seen as being a bit different and therefore a little more creative than the usual fare. It can be fraught with difficulties, however. I usually find that one of the panel hogs the limelight, speaks far too long and leaves little room for anyone else's opinion. What is needed is a highly competent chair or moderator who controls the proceedings, keeps a tight rein on speakers and time alike, and facilitates any interaction with the audience. If you are guaranteed a strong panel chair, it can be a good way of breaking up a succession of solo presentations, so I would recommend it with reservations. Of course you can turn this on its head. If you are asked to speak at a conference, you might suggest doing the session as a panel discussion, though again, make sure you have someone keeping control. Or setting your presentation up as an interview can also work well, though you do need to rehearse together and make sure that the interviewer knows how to pose a question that doesn't sound false. If you have a colleague with journalistic or broadcasting experience, they will probably have the requisite skills.

Interacting with Your Audience

In the example of the moneybags above, the speaker both used props and interacted with his audience, and this

80

interaction is well worth exploring. If you are asked to give a presentation, does the communication have to be one way? Does it have to be just you, standing on a stage, speaking for twenty minutes and then possibly inviting questions? Why not get the audience doing something? If they are sitting cabaret-style, as they were with the moneybags example, get them discussing an issue themselves for a few minutes and then have them report back. This needs careful handling, by the way, so do this with caution. Your role has changed from that of speaker to facilitator, and you need to be aware of the difference.

Get Them Doing Something

It can often be a good idea to get an audience to put their hands in the air. You might ask who supports one side of an argument – 'hands up those who would ban fox hunting!' Or perhaps you are talking about change and how uncomfortable it can be: 'Everybody, please sit with your feet on the ground and your hands on your knees. Now cross your legs. Now cross your arms. Now cross your legs the other way. Now cross your arms the other way.' Try it yourself – you'll almost certainly find that you feel perfectly comfortable crossing your legs both ways, though crossing your arms in a way that is different from your norm will feel strange and uncomfortable. And if changing something so simple can feel uncomfortable, think how uncomfortable a major change in processes or structure will feel. Nevertheless, you **could** cross your arms the other way, uncomfortable as it was, and so you will be just as capable of coping with a more substantial change as well – including changing the way you do your presentations! All such physical activities also have the advantage of making your audience move around a bit, and so (hopefully) encouraging them to be more alert.

You might try sticking something under the audience's chairs, ready for the appropriate moment in your presentation. This needs the cooperation of the organiser (if it is at a conference, of course) yet it can be quite a *coup de théâtre*: '*If you care to feel under your seat, in amongst the hardened blobs of age-old chewing gum, you'll find an envelope. If you would open it and take out what's inside, then I'll tell you what to do with it.*' I remember a friend of mine doing this at a conference. Inside the envelopes were three pieces of paper, one with two pictures of riders and two with pictures of horses, and the audience members had to see if they could fit the riders on the horses – the point being that the answer is not obvious and is, in fact, counter-intuitive.

You will find many examples of this very old puzzle if you google 'horse and rider puzzle'.

Of course, you could put something more dramatic under their chairs – perhaps djembe drums, kazoos, or 'found' instruments (ie, bits of tube and plastic and so on that can be blown into, shaken or struck to make a noise) so that they are ready for you to conduct them in a rousing rendition of the 'Skye Boat Song' or 'Frère Jacques'. I've had the pleasure of running a session with the help of a chamber orchestra at a conference looking at leadership and teamwork. I gave the orchestra and the conductor a piece of music they had never seen before, and explored with the audience how the players rehearsed together, how they were led, what happened when things changed (I took the conductor away, for example, and got someone from the audience to come up and conduct in his place) and so on; and I have done similar sessions with a string quartet, which is rather less expensive! And I've seen a speaker on teamwork teach the audience an African chant which they could sing in four-part harmony within twenty minutes.

Using Actors

Or have you considered using actors to perform a scene that illustrates some of the points you wish to make? At one conference, instead of having yet another PowerPoint-dominated presentation, this time on the subject of the new Corporate Manslaughter legislation, we acted out a situation which showed how a sequence of apparently innocuous decisions made by the director of housing at a local authority could lead to a disaster which could in turn have resulted in a charge of corporate manslaughter. Acting it out was much more telling than just talking about it. At the same conference, two delegates (played by actors, of course), came in just as the event was starting, talking loudly about how awful the previous year's conference had been. The conference host was then able to assure the audience that this year was going to be different. . . .

Make Sure You are Comfortable with Your Ideas

All these last ideas require you to be experts in the relevant field, so I am not suggesting that you try to tackle these sorts of art-based interventions in a presentation unless you are yourself highly competent – and if you are, you probably don't need to be reading this book. I include them to make the point that there is no limit to how creative you can be in your presentations if you apply your imagination.

Key Points to Remember

* Stories and metaphors will always make your presentation more creative and interesting.

* Props and audience interaction can also work well to make your speech memorable.

* There is no limit to your ability to come up with new and creative ways of presenting to an audience.

---

5. Language in Brilliant Speeches

Although I have explored how to devise the content and structure of your presentation, I have hardly touched on the words to use. This chapter is all about language in brilliant speeches, and if you follow its advice, your words will ring in the ears of your audience long after you have finished speaking.

What's in this Chapter?

* Using simple English (and no jargon)
* Using powerful, descriptive English
* Concrete nouns and active verbs
* The use of pronouns
* Rhetorical devices such as alliteration and anaphora
* Using quotations.

Short Words and Common Words

Many of the best speeches use short words in common use so that the audience is never in doubt as to what is being said. Winston Churchill was a master of this: *'We shall fight in France. We shall fight on the seas and oceans. We shall fight with growing confidence and growing strength in the air. We shall defend our island, whatever the cost may be. We shall fight on the beaches. We shall fight on the landing grounds. We shall fight in the fields and in the streets. We shall fight in the hills. We shall never surrender.'*

Only two words in that extract, *'confidence'* and *'surrender'*, have more than two syllables, and neither is unusual.

Short Sentences Work in Spoken English

I often find I need to get participants on my courses to speak in shorter sentences. Many of them keep on going, adding subordinate clause after subordinate clause until the sense and impact are lost in the mists of time. Dare to reach a full stop. Breathe! Pause! You don't have to speak in grammatically correct sentences in a speech. Indeed, often a couple of words will do: *'The competition are at the gates. Battering them down. Thud! There's their battering ram! And another. Thud!*

No Jargon

The Plain English Campaign quotes some wonderful examples of long, complicated sentences riddled with abstract words, which can so easily be said simply. Here's one example from their website (www.plainenglish.co.uk/examples.html):

'High quality learning environments are a necessary precondition for facilitation and enhancement of the ongoing learning process.'

Their suggested improvement is:

'Children need good schools if they are to learn properly.'

The Prevalence of Corporate-Speak

Many organisations have made concerted efforts to improve, yet you can still easily find official documents with sentences like this (and this is a very tame example – there are many more extreme ones):

'To maintain full cover, we would ask that your remittance be received within the next seven days.'

Financial institutions such as banks and insurance companies seem to be particularly prone to this sort of language. Note how they use an obscure word like 'remittance' and how they have turned the sentence, rather clumsily, into the passive tense. Yet imagine an evening when you have gone out for dinner with friends and have forgotten your wallet. Would you say to the friend who pays for your dinner, *'I'll ensure that my remittance is received by you'*? Of course not. You'd say something like *'Thanks so much, Bob, I'll pop a cheque in the post.'*

The problem is that this sort of corporate-speak is contagious and most of the business world now suffers from it. Often, I suspect, this is the result of 'legalese', words that employees have been told to say (or, more usually, write) so as to reduce the chance that the company may be held liable for some failure or other. Or is it management jargon that has led to clichés like *'thinking outside the box'*, *'mission critical'* and *'pushing the envelope'* being used *ad nauseam*? What does *'pushing the envelope'* mean? I have no idea, and I suspect most of the people who hear it at work don't know either.

Some of these management clichés were once powerful metaphors, though they have lost all their impact and often their meaning through overuse. So, generally, it is a good idea to avoid them, though some, like 'the elephant in the room', seem to me to have a bit of life left in them. At least those words are simple, and the image is graphic.

Not Only Short, Common Words

None of this means that you must never use longer or more unusual words. On the contrary, if all you use is plain English, your presentation runs the risk of sounding very dull. To mix my metaphors unashamedly, you should pepper your speech with occasional words and phrases that sit up and beg to be noticed.

A good example of this is General MacArthur's farewell to the Corps of Cadets at West Point in 1962. You might have thought a soldier would have said something fairly prosaic and down to earth, such as:

'I am getting on now and am about to retire. I have some wonderful memories of my career and I know I am going to miss things like reveille and the drums. I can still hear the sound of the guns and the noise of the battlefield in my head. But as I grow older, I keep remembering West Point and the things I was taught here.'

Not General MacArthur, though. What he said was:

'The shadows are lengthening for me. The twilight is here. My days of old have vanished. They have gone glimmering through the dreams of things that were. Their memory is one of wondrous beauty, watered by tears and coaxed and caressed by the smiles of yesterday. I listen, then, but with thirsty ear, for the witching melody of faint bugles blowing reveille, of far drums beating the long roll. In my dreams I hear again the crash of guns, the rattle of musketry, the strange, mournful chatter of the battlefield. But in the evening of my memory, I come back to West Point. Always there echoes and re-echoes: duty, honour, country.'

This starts very simply yet it soon dives into a sea of metaphor in which language is used brilliantly. Don't you love *'the witching melody of faint bugles blowing reveille'*, *'coaxed and caressed by the smiles of yesterday'* and *'the strange, mournful chatter of the battlefield'*?

If he had taken the prosaic approach, the effect would have been minimal. Great soldier that he was, General MacArthur clearly had the soul of a poet.

Have Fun with Words

We are not all poets, of course, and much of what we are asked to speak about may seem very commonplace if not downright dull. Nevertheless, playing around with language can reap great rewards. Have fun with words. Puns (not too cringe-worthy though) and rhymes can really bring your speeches to life, and audiences love them. Think of the classic Two Ronnies sketch *'Four Candles'* and the way that they played with language in that, and in many of their other sketches. Or you may remember a line from that ineffably silly sitcom, *'Allo 'Allo*, in which René, the café patron, was discussing killing the General, and came up with this line: *'Do you not see, if we kill him with the pill from the till by mixing with it the drug from the jug, we need not light the candle with the handle on the gateau from the chateau.'* Daft, yet inspired.

I am not suggesting that you can become a brilliant scriptwriter overnight; rather that playing with language and keeping your mind open to opportunities for rhymes and puns and other plays on words can transform your presentation from the mind-numbing to the mind-blowing.

Active Verbs and Vivid Nouns

The best speeches use active verbs and vivid nouns. It is much better to say *'We must jump some pretty high hurdles if we are to win this race'* than *'There are considerable challenges to be met.'* Much better to say *'If we don't boost sales, we'll bleed to death'* than *'If we don't increase our sales figures, there will be a steady decline in our commercial viability.'* Much better to cheer than congratulate, to bang rather than go off, to ooze than to emerge.

Aim for the Concrete, Not the Abstract

This is the sort of thing many managers will say in a presentation:

'We must continually strive for sales effectiveness and operational excellence.'

The sentiment is clear but the language is not inspirational. This is not going to motivate an audience of salespeople to redouble their efforts. Part of the problem is that words like 'effectiveness' and 'excellence' are abstract. Try turning those words into concrete images:

'We've all got to aim at a tough sales target. I don't want us aiming just anywhere on that target; we're going to be so good at how we sell that nothing but the bull's-eye will do.'

There is nothing special in this example. People often talk about sales targets, so the concept will be very familiar to the audience. Yet *'target'* is a much more concrete word than 'effectiveness' or 'excellence', and all I have done is make it slightly more concrete by talking about a bull's-eye. Any business audience would be able to equate hitting the bull's-eye with the highest standards. You could easily expand the metaphor to include inners and outers, or talk about 'taking careful aim' rather than 'drawing a bow at a venture'.

Adjectives Add Colour and Emotion

Adjectives, though perhaps not as crucial as nouns and verbs, also have an important role to play. They will often add colour and emotion to an otherwise dull speech. They can also really help an audience visualise what you are talking about and, as I have already said, most of us think in pictures. If you say '*I want a quick, efficient response to new sales leads*', you are being very clear yet the adjectives are not inspiring. How about 'a fierce response'? Or even 'a tigerish response'? Perhaps you could change it round and 'gobble up new sales leads like a tiger'; a powerful verb and a strong noun and a simile instead of an adjective.

General MacArthur's use of the word '*mournful*' to describe the chatter of gunfire on the battlefield is inspired. A participant on a recent course, describing a situation that had upset her, said '*I was disturbed, disgusted and depressed*' – a lovely use of powerful adjectives, **and** alliteration **and** the 'Rule of Three', all in one go. (I discuss the 'Rule of Three' and alliteration below.) Incidentally, the occasional dip into Roget's Thesaurus to find alternative words to the ones that initially spring to mind can be an invaluable aid.

I don't generally recommend scattering adjectives around like confetti, though; use them judiciously and try to avoid always employing the lacklustre ones like 'nice', 'good', 'bad', 'great', and even 'interesting' and 'exciting' which are used so often that they seem to have lost any power they once had.

Make Your Pronouns Work for You (Or Them, Or Us)

Pronouns have a particularly important part to play in good speeches. Think about your objective. Are you perhaps urging a group of people to work more collaboratively? Then use '**we**' a lot to create a sense of unity and togetherness. Do you need to reach out to your audience and appeal to their common cause? Talk about '**you**'. Is there a lot of competition out there? Talk about '**they**' and '**them**' – or, better still, talk about '**them**' and '**us**'. And if you want to underline that you are the one in charge, talk about '**I**' and '**me**'. Remember Churchill's *'We will fight them. . .'*? He emphasised the unity of purpose and the common enemy very clearly through the repetition of those two pronouns.

Anaphora, or Deliberate Repetition

There are many rhetorical devices, often identified by the ancient Greeks who made rhetoric into an art form, that still persist effectively today. Winston Churchill's *'We will fight them. . .'* and Martin Luther King's *'I have a dream. . .'* speeches are both great examples of 'anaphora' or deliberate repetition of a phrase. If you want to re-emphasise a point, find a neat way of saying it and then repeat the same phrase throughout your speech. The audience will go away with those words ringing in their ears. This works effectively when repeating the phrase at the end of a sentence as well (when it is technically known as 'epiphora', just in case you'd like to know).

The Rule of Three

I mentioned above the 'Rule of Three', which came up in our original list of Essences of Powerful Communication. The Rule of Three is one of those magical rhetorical devices that works, though no one quite knows why. The principle is simple – if you are going to use a list of examples, use three. If you are going to use a series of descriptive adjectives, use three. Four is too many, two doesn't quite seem enough. Gardeners know to plant the same flowers in groups of three as the human eye seems to see this as an integrated whole whereas it will split groups of four into two twos.

Groups of three are commonplace in many of our cultural references, from the 'Father, Son and Holy Spirit' of the Anglican Church, to the classic start to a joke (now rather frowned upon) *'There was an Englishman, a Scotsman and an Irishman. . .'* In classic tales, the Rule of Three is common – the hero(ine) can have three wishes, has to rub the lamp three times, has three attempts to solve a riddle. Think of Goldilocks and the Three Bears, the Three Little Pigs, and the Three Blind Mice. Consider *'On your Marks, Get Set, Go!'* Or *'Life, liberty and the pursuit of happiness'*, or *'Government of the people, by the people, for the people.'* Or *'Faith, hope and charity'.*

In comedy, two is the minimum number required to convey a pattern, and the third element is often a deliberate contrast or a twist designed to evoke laughter. This is a classic example of this: *'There are three kinds of untruths: lies, damned lies and statistics.'* Or how about *'I find it quite easy to pack for a weekend in the country – Barbour, wellies, machine gun.'* In this case, both the rhythm and the surprise last item make the joke work.

More Rhetorical Devices

There are many other rhetorical devices to try. Anticlimax involves moving from a significant point to a commonplace one. Like the Rule of Three, this is often used by writers (such as Woody Allen) for comic effect: *'Not only is there no God, but try getting a plumber on weekends.'* Its close cousin is 'antithesis' which means using contrasting words or phrases, and there are many telling examples of this:

'One small step for a man, one giant leap for mankind.'

'To err is human; to forgive, divine.'

Barack Obama (or his scriptwriter) is particularly fond of antithesis:

'. . .*in a way that heals, not in a way that wounds.*' And in his election night speech in 2012: '*Tonight you voted for action, not politics as usual. You elected us to focus on your jobs, not ours.*'

Other rhetorical devices include 'onomatopoeia' (using words that sound like what they mean – '*snap, crackle, pop*') and 'alliteration' (using words that start with the same letter or sounds). It is much more powerful to talk about the '*dark days of December*' than just '*December*'. David Cameron, not always a great speaker, did come up with a fine example of alliteration some years ago:

'*The details are damning. A fragmented family held together by drink, drugs and deception. An estate where decency fights a losing battle against degradation and despair.*'

Balancing Emotion and Logic

It is important to stress that colourful and emotionally charged language should not be used at the expense of logic and even interesting facts. There is a balance to be found. The best speeches speak both to the heart and to the mind. If you concentrate solely on appealing to the mind and speak only of dreary facts, your message may be clear and logical but no one will be listening and you will inspire the audience to no action at all. Many business people think this is the right way because it seems to be 'businesslike' – analytical, data-oriented, factual.

But such speakers fail to engage the right hand side of their audience's brains, the part that deals with emotion, beliefs, values, intuition. On the other hand, flowery, emotional language without content or rationale will quickly sound empty and you will come across as a showman, all mouth and no trousers. The language that you use as a speaker needs to connect with both sides of the brain.

'I Have a Dream. . .'

I have quoted at some length from a number of famous speeches in this chapter, and have referred to others. The one I have referred to without quoting at any length is Martin Luther King's famous speech calling for an end to racism in America, *'I have a dream. . .'* which he delivered to a mass rally in Washington in 1963. In case you don't know it (and many of the younger generation today, perhaps not surprisingly, don't), here is an extract:

I am not unmindful that some of you have come here out of great trials and tribulations. Some of you have come fresh from narrow cells. Some of you have come from areas where your quest for freedom left you battered by the storms of persecution and staggered by the winds of police brutality. You have been the veterans of creative suffering. Continue to work with the faith that unearned suffering is redemptive.

'Go back to Mississippi, go back to Alabama, go back to Georgia, go back to Louisiana, go back to the slums and ghettos of our northern cities, knowing that somehow this situation can and will be changed. Let us not wallow in the valley of despair.

'I say to you today, my friends, that in spite of the difficulties and frustrations of the moment, I still have a dream. It is a dream deeply rooted in the American dream.

'I have a dream that one day this nation will rise up and live out the true meaning of its creed: "We hold these truths to be self-evident; that all men are created equal". I have a dream that one day on the red hills of Georgia the sons of former slaves and the sons of former slave-owners will be able to sit down together at a table of brotherhood.

'I have a dream that one day even the state of Mississippi, a desert state, sweltering with the heat of injustice and oppression, will be transformed into an oasis of freedom and justice.

'I have a dream that my four children will one day live in a nation where they will not be judged by the colour of their skin but by the content of their character. I have a dream today.'

Powerful stuff.

Using Quotations

A couple of pointers about using quotations in your own speeches. These can be very effective provided they are punchy and completely relevant, and provided too that you don't try to pass them off as your own. Joe Biden, in his quest to become US President in 1988, famously quoted, with minor alterations, from a speech given by Neil Kinnock, the ex-Labour leader, but failed to credit him, with the result that Biden himself was discredited and his campaign imploded. (In fact, Biden **had** credited Kinnock when he used the same words before, but on this one occasion he didn't, and the media picked it up.)

It also helps if the person you cite is well known. I once made a speech in which I quoted: '*All great discoveries are made by people whose feelings run ahead of their thoughts.*' This was apparently said by someone called C. H. Oakhurst, and I had no idea who he was, though I liked the quotation. My answer to this dilemma was to confess that I didn't know who C. H. Oakhurst was and to ask the audience to tell me if they did. No one else knew either (and I still don't). Incidentally, speaking at a conference, I once quoted some research about powers of creativity diminishing as you grow older. I explained that I was sorry, but I didn't know who had undertaken the research. At that moment, a voice from the audience floated up: '*I did.*' His name was Kobus Neethling, and we had a very entertaining conversation afterwards!

The lesson is to cite your sources or confess that you don't know who came up with the quote in the first place.

Succinct, Convincing and Relevant

Some quotations get overused – they were mostly said by Einstein – because they are so succinct and convincing; and **succinct** and **convincing** are two key essentials of a good quotation to go with **relevant**. Don't use too many – the audience generally wants to hear what you have to say, not what some long-dead sage said, however brilliantly they put it. If you are going to use quotations, use them judiciously.

Key Points to Remember

* If in doubt, use simple, jargon-free English.

* Spice up your speeches by using punchy, unusual words and phrases.

* Rhetorical devices such as metaphor, the Rule of Three, and anaphora work, so use them.

---

6. Practice Makes Perfect

This short chapter is all about the importance of rehearsal and how to do it properly. If you follow the advice, I promise your speeches will be dramatically improved.

What's in this Chapter?

* How professional performers rehearse
* 'Putting it on its feet'
* The benefits of feedback
* New ideas, phrases and gestures come from rehearsal
* The importance of muscle memory
* Rehearsal might change everything you have prepared so far
* Thinking, writing and speaking use different parts of the brain.

Knowing What You Want to Say is Not the Same as Rehearsing

I am often asked to coach managers who have an important presentation coming up. Usually, I am brought in a little bit too late in the process, once they have 'written' their speech and are now panicking about the delivery. I often ask: *'What have you prepared?'* and they tell me *'Oh, I know what I want to say.'* Leaving aside the point that what they want to say may well not be what the audience wants or needs to hear, at this point I tell them *'Okay, so you have prepared about ten per cent of what you need to.'*

This comes as a shock to most people – they know what they want to say, so surely they are nearly there? In reality, they are nowhere near ready.

How Do Actors Rehearse?

Think of a theatre company coming together to rehearse Hamlet, or any play, it doesn't matter which. The words are written down – the actors know what the author wanted to say. By the end of the first week of rehearsal, the actors will know their lines off by heart; and then they will spend three, four, sometimes six or seven weeks more, rehearsing **how to say** those lines.

In Hamlet, of course, part of that time will be spent choreographing fights, deciding how to get the ghost of Hamlet's father to come on stage, and how to stab Polonius through a curtain. You probably won't be including such things in your speech.

Much of the time, though, will be spent playing around with how each line is said. Actors will try it one way and then another, all the time slowly building a performance that has the impact that they and the director (and the author, one hopes) are seeking. It is a process of iteration and reiteration, gradually adding layers of subtlety and meaning and impact to each actor's performance until it is ready for an audience. Of course, it is about more than the words alone. Gesture, facial expression, movement and many other non-verbal elements are equally important.

Putting It On Its Feet

One of the key things about rehearsal is that it is not a predominantly cerebral process. That is, actors don't sit around discussing how to do it, though they could do. Instead, they stand up and say the lines out loud – in theatre jargon, they 'put it on its feet'. I am not suggesting that actors and directors do not think about the lines; on the contrary, they often go into great depths of analysis. Yet they know that it is by standing up and actually speaking the lines that they will most effectively find out the best way to say them.

Business people should learn from this. So many of the executives I coach imagine that working out what they want to say and then thinking their speech through in their heads is enough. It isn't. They have to put it on its feet.

I wrote earlier that making a great speech requires learning a new skill, and it is fundamentally a practical skill. You cannot learn a practical skill in theory – you have to put it into practice. You cannot learn how to juggle or ride a bike by reading a description of how to do it – you have to try it yourself. You have to learn what it feels like to wobble and fall off, or to drop those juggling balls and pick them up again. This is why I am so insistent with my course delegates that they should put their speech on its feet. Try it out, don't just think it through.

Sometimes, a manager will tell me '*I run through it in front of the bathroom mirror.*' This is better, though not much.

Part of the problem is that many people think that if they say words out loud, apparently to no one, they will look stupid. There are two possible answers to this. One is to find a quiet place where no one will see or overhear you. The other is to persuade a colleague or friend or partner to sit and listen and give some feedback. Of these, the first is better than nothing, and the second is much the best way.

The Benefits of Feedback

On presentation skills courses, I often give each participant a twenty- to thirty-minute slot to present a short (two-minute) speech to me and a small group of other participants so we can give everyone individual feedback. Almost without exception, everyone makes a quantum leap in quality and impact. I get them to start again, stop them, try it an alternative way, try it with more energy, try it going 'over the top', try it **with** movement or gesture, try it **without**, try it with a different emphasis on particular words, try it with different words altogether. And they get more suggestions from their colleagues, too. Finally, they are rehearsing, properly rehearsing.

It is a tough process and sometimes participants feel as though their head is exploding, yet the improvement they make in those short twenty-minute slots is remarkable.

New Ideas, Phrases and Gestures Come from Rehearsal

Going through this process, I often find that new phrases or gestures or ideas suddenly spring to the mind of the speaker. One course participant recently found himself saying: '*We need proper printers, not problem printers.*' A lovely phrase, and it came completely out of the blue. Another one, talking about meaningless conversations, made a tiny motion with her fingers and thumb, just a twitch, really, and I got her to make it a big, clear, bold gesture with both hands. Now her hands were yakking away at each other, and her body was telling the story. She had the instinctive desire to make the gesture, she just needed the feedback to get her to make it effective.

The Importance of Muscle Memory

Not only does rehearsal trigger new ideas, it also helps form 'muscle memory'. Try saying that quirky, alliterative phrase above: 'We want proper printers, not problem printers.' It's a bit of a tongue-twister, and the more you practice it, the more clearly you will be able to say it – and it needs clarity to have its full effect. The muscles in your mouth will have got used to saying it.

Of course your mouth will also have got used to saying a whole load of business-specific jargon that you and your colleagues are used to, though your audience may not be. Perhaps you use the phrase 'A trace system pixel data interface' on a regular basis (I hope you don't as I just made it up). If so, you probably garble it so much that an outsider wouldn't have a clue what you are saying. Again, putting your presentation on its feet and getting a friendly colleague to listen to you should highlight these sorts of errors. Then you can practise saying the phrase in question clearly and confidently, and your mouth muscles will remember how to articulate it properly when you finally come to say it in your presentation.

Rehearsing Properly Might Mean Changing Your Structure. . .

The third good reason for properly rehearsing your presentation is that by speaking it out loud, you often find that the order you have put things in doesn't make sense. Perhaps you set out with a clear plan in your head – B follows A and in turns leads on to C, D and E. When you put it on its feet for the first time, you may well find that D comes before C and, hold on, what are P and H doing in there? You included them because at the time, in the moment, it seemed the right thing to do. The logical through line that you have in your head (or, if you have written it down, on the page) may seem quite illogical when you actually come to deliver it. Thinking, writing and speaking are different processes, using different parts of your brain, and you need to find a sequence for your presentation that works when you speak it, not when you write or think it.

. . .Or Changing Your Words

The same thing applies to turns of phrase. Often, words look fine on paper or even sound okay in your head, though they are terribly clunky when you come to speak them. This is particularly so of people who suffer from corporate-speak (and that means most people in business). They become so used to reading official company letters, reports, contracts and so on that they regurgitate them in their speeches. I teased one participant on a course who talked about an 'ingress of water', a phrase that came up regularly in her work and, admittedly, had a specific meaning.

'Would you use that phrase over a dinner table with your friends?' I asked. *'Would you say "Oh, we're having terrible trouble with our roof, we are suffering from an ingress of water"?'*

Of course, if your audience is made up of close colleagues, they may well not notice such corporate jargon, as they are probably infected themselves. Equally, they may not notice you saying *'yourself'* or *'themselves'* when you should say *'you'* and *'them'* or when you put an 'H' on the letter 'aitch' – particularly common when people talk about HR and pronounce it Haitch R!

So, put it on its feet.

Memorising Your Speech

You may feel that you have a poor memory and so must have a script or detailed notes to refer to. On my courses, when participants are at the early stages of developing a presentation, I often allow them to refer to their Post-it note structure or use notes with bullet points. However, as you refine and develop your presentation through rehearsal, you will find that phrases and whole sentences will begin to stick in your mind, and you are well on your way to memorising the whole thing. If you don't rehearse enough, you are very unlikely to be able to remember it all.

If you are really worried about forgetting what you wanted to say, use notes. For a long presentation, this is entirely acceptable. If you do use notes, though, write them on cards, not paper, as paper has a tendency to flutter and shake and catch the eye, particularly if you are nervous. Plain postcards (about fifteen centimetres by ten centimetres) work well as they are small enough to be unobtrusive and yet large enough for you to read. I recommend using one postcard for each section of your presentation, with a heading and a few bullet points to remind you of the salient points within that section. If you find you need to write down whole sentences, stop. If they are that important, learn them off by heart.

If it is very important that you say the right things in the right way in a particular speech, you may feel that you want to write it out in full. If you do, it doesn't preclude the need for rehearsal; nor does it allow you just to read your speech as though you were reading the lesson in church. Practise delivering the speech while hardly glancing at the words. Maintain eye contact with the audience as much as possible, and if you do need to look down, look up again straight afterwards. To get this right is not easy, so you need to rehearse just as much to make reading a speech work well, even if you have the comfort of knowing your lines are in front of you.

It is more effective to do without notes if you can, of course. Once you have your structure set and the various subsections well-established, you could try finding a mnemonic to help you remember at least the overall structure. Perhaps you are preparing a speech about health and safety. Your opening might be an 'earthquake' about the importance of avoiding **D**eath. Then you go on to talk about the **A**ntipathy that exists in many organisations towards health and safety. Perhaps your next section is about **R**isk, followed by one on **W**orkplace safety. And maybe you will end with a section stressing the need for **I**magination in assessing risk including a final story about the **N**itwit who electrocuted himself. Remembering DARWIN gives you all the headings for your six sections.

Or you might try associating the various sections of your presentation with stages in a journey, which can work well since you need to take your audience on this journey with you. Connect each section of your speech with a place on your journey and visualise it clearly in your mind. Once you can remember the stages of your journey, and even the milestones in between, you will have the skeleton of your speech memorised.

There are many other ways of helping you to remember

your presentation, but these two simple tools seem to work for most people. Bear in mind, though, that nothing beats good, thorough rehearsal for helping you remember a speech.

Key Points to Remember

* If you haven't rehearsed your speech properly you are nowhere near ready to deliver it.

* You cannot rehearse your presentation in your head, you must get up and speak it out loud.

* Get a colleague or friend to give you some feedback so you know how you are coming across.

---

7. Preparing for a Presentation

This chapter is all about making sure you are as ready as you can be to deliver a great speech. It's about how to prepare yourself physically, vocally, mentally and practically so that when you get up to speak, you are performing at your best.

What's in this Chapter?

* Preparation matters
* A tale of the unexpected
* Who are your audience?
* Dealing with the practicalities
* Preparing yourself physically, vocally and mentally
* Avoiding tension
* Breathing well and deeply
* Performing at your best
* Vocal mechanics.

How Professionals Prepare

I once heard an eminent golfer talking about what it was

like to tee off at seven o'clock in the morning, a start time that is quite normal in big professional tournaments. He said *'I get up at half past four so I can eat a good breakfast – after all, I shall be walking over five miles, up hill and down dale, this morning – and then I get to the course at half past five so that I can warm up on the range. I need to loosen up physically, sniff the air, settle myself down, get a feel for the way the course is looking, see the spectators arriving, prepare myself physically and mentally, so that when it comes to my first drive of the day, I am completely and totally ready.'*

Most professional performers – actors, dancers, musicians – do the same. A ballerina will probably do an hour of physical warm-up exercises before a performance, as she knows that unless she does so, she is likely to fall flat on her face – literally. Brass players simply cannot make a decent sound unless they have warmed themselves and their instruments up. If you are presenting, your body is your instrument. In fact, that's rather a good way of considering yourself – as a wind instrument.

Some of the content of this chapter might seem obvious, particularly the practical points, yet I have experienced speakers falling down over every single one of these, so it seems worth reiterating them. Some of these matters, of course, you may not be able to influence, though that doesn't mean that it is not worth considering them in advance.

A Tale of the Unexpected

I once telephoned someone I had been coaching to ask how a presentation had gone, and he said *'I couldn't believe it, there were three hundred people there!'*

'I thought you said it would be for fifty,' I said.

'That's what I thought, but I was wrong.'

'So what happened?'

'Well, I had expected them to be sitting at tables, cabaret-style, you remember, we spoke about getting them to confer on their tables. . .'

'Yes, I remember.'

'Well, it didn't work when they were all sitting in serried rows.'

'I can see that might have made it difficult,' I said.

'And the only part of the stage that was lit was a lectern as they were obviously expecting me to have PowerPoint slides. And they didn't give me a lapel microphone so I had to stay behind the lectern. And my mouth went dry, and my brain froze and I could tell they were all shuffling about and getting embarrassed. It was a disaster.'

Indeed it was a disaster, and the sad thing was that he had rehearsed his speech really thoroughly and stood every chance of wowing his audience. But he hadn't checked the practicalities.

Who Are Your Audience?

So let's start with the audience. If you are preparing to make a speech to colleagues at work, you will probably know who and how many will be there. If you have been asked to present to an external audience, you need to check.

How many will there be? Who are they? What is their background? What do they know? What are they expecting from you? I have already stressed the importance of thinking in advance what the audience needs and wants to know, as it will undoubtedly affect what you say. If you don't know even the most basic things about your prospective audience, how are you going to be able to work out what they need or want to know?

Consider also whether you know any of the audience. If you do, a phone call to your contact in advance may allow you to get more of a handle on who the audience will be, or give you some other insight into the issues concerning them. Just knowing that there is a friendly face in the audience can make a huge difference to you.

Where Are You Going to be Speaking?

What about the venue? Do you know where it is? Can you park? Don't laugh – a friend of mine had been asked to speak at a conference at a rural hotel. First off, he was later than he intended as he couldn't find the place (this was in the days before sat nav) and then he couldn't find a free space in the car park. Eventually, in desperation, he parked in a space designated for disabled drivers and rushed into the conference centre, hot and flustered, just a few minutes before he was due to go on. He told the receptionist why he had parked in a disabled bay, but he still came out later to find his car clamped. Not a good day.

What Equipment Will You be Expected to Use?

What equipment will be available to you? Will there be a projector (if you are still wedded to slides)? Is it back-projection? What about microphones? Will there be a sound specialist there to mike you up? Will you have a chance to test the mike?

Make Sure the Light Shines on You

What will the lighting be like? Will everyone be able to see you? Will you be able to see them? Can you adjust the lighting? I regularly work for one company which has an auditorium with raked seating for internal seminars and conferences. There are a few preordained lighting settings from which to choose, though none of them sheds any reasonable light on anyone standing on the stage. There are some small spotlights in the ceiling over the stage, yet all they do is light the top of your head, leaving your face in shadow. The whole auditorium was designed exclusively for PowerPoint presentations, with the expectation that the speaker will stand behind a lectern to the side of the stage. As you will have gathered if you have read the rest of this book, this is not a style of presentation that I would recommend to anyone, so all the managers I have coached at that company now find that their auditorium is the last place in which they want to present.

How Will the Seating be Arranged?

That auditorium has fixed seats on raked rows, which is really not great if you want your audience to get up and do something (inter)active. Do check in advance how the seating will be arranged and whether the seats can be moved. I once got caught out by this myself. I asked the venue if the seats were fixed and got told 'no', only to find when I arrived that although the seats were not permanently fixed, they linked together, so people couldn't just move their seats without unlinking the whole row. So that blew that plan. . . Perhaps the seating doesn't take up all the room and there is space behind them in which you could get the audience doing something active – there wasn't in my case.

Getting a Feel for the Room

And crucially, can you do a dry run *in situ*? You may be the third person to speak that morning, so find out what time you need to be there so you can check out the stage, get a feel for the room and the acoustic, ask for some feedback as to whether you are too loud or too soft, too quick or slow, clearly seen or invisible and so on. Remember that the room will feel different when it is full of people, so try to bear that in mind. It particularly affects the acoustics, since the human body *en masse* tends to absorb a lot of sound.

No actor would appear on a stage without having explored it first, got a sense of its scale and its relationship with the audience, felt the temperature and the humidity, worked out how to get on and off and so on. And nor should you.

Make Friends with the Organiser

Whoever is organising this event should be your key ally in all this, and in the question of timings. How long have you got? Are you expected to speak for the whole of your allocated time or can you leave time for questions or a discussion? Is there a coffee or lunch break immediately before or after your session? If there is a break just before you go on, it helps enormously in that you will have time to test out the stage, get miked up and so on. And if you immediately precede a break, be aware that this may affect people's concentration – they may well be thirsty, hungry or dying for the loo.

Prepare for the Unexpected

And finally in this practical section, it can help to have a few ideas of what to do if something outside your control goes wrong. Perhaps you have prepared those dreaded PowerPoint slides and the projector breaks down; or perhaps your laptop is incompatible with the equipment at the venue – not unheard of. What if the fire alarm goes off, or the lights fuse? What are you going to do? Can you turn a disaster into a triumph? The first rule is to keep calm, of course. Decide whether you should be carrying on regardless – yes, if it is a PowerPoint malfunction; no, if it is a fire!

What will you do if the organiser asks you to cut down your speech (or, rarely, to expand it) just as you are about to go on?

I had to cope with something like this some years ago when I was asked to speak at a conference in Paris – in French. In the dim and distant past, my French had been pretty good, but I was very rusty. I learnt most of the language while studying at university and as a teacher in a lycée in Lot et Garonne many years before; I could quote bits of Racine and Corneille and fluently exhort a rowdy class of fourteen-year-olds to calm down, though my business vocabulary was minimal. So I had carefully prepared and even written out large chunks of my speech.

I was due to share the platform with two other speakers (both native French) in the session immediately after lunch. While we were eating, the charming but rather scatty conference organiser sat down at our table and announced that she wanted us to depart from our prepared speeches and cover a rather different subject. She dismissed my protestations, saying that I spoke excellent French and that no one would mind if I made the odd grammatical error, and before I knew it, the session was starting and I was on. And I was the first to speak. I did the only thing I could think of which was to start my presentation by recounting what had happened over lunch, and explaining that therefore I had no speech to make. And at that point I took 'my speech' (actually a spare piece of paper), crumpled it up and ruefully tossed it over my shoulder. That at least got a laugh and I felt the audience were on my side, so I then stumbled through an off-the-cuff presentation, occasionally becoming more fluent as I found a way of bringing in sections of the speech I had prepared. It was not brilliant, though I had survived.

When the Unexpected Helped

The lesson of this story is to expect the unexpected and plan for it. Sometimes the unexpected works in your favour. I was coaching two managers who had been asked to speak at a conference for insurance brokers. They were from one of ten insurance companies invited to speak at twenty-five-minute break-out sessions, and they were due to repeat the same presentation five times on the first afternoon and five more times the following day. They had been told that they would be allocated a room and could expect an audience of thirty-odd at each session. Since I was coaching them for their presentation, we quickly abandoned PowerPoint for a more creative and interactive approach (with one of them pretending to be a member of the audience, at least to start with), and this decision played into their hands. The conference organisers suddenly realised that it made much more sense to move a few speakers from room to room than to try to shift three hundred delegates all at the same time. Unfortunately for them, the other speakers had all come with their PowerPoint presentations prepared which meant that at the end of their sessions, they had to unplug their laptops, move to another room, connect their laptops to new projectors, warm them up and so on, with the result that half their available time was used up dealing with the technology. My two PowerPointless presenters could saunter to their new room and deliver their whole presentation without feeling rushed. The outcome was

122

that by the last few break-out sessions on the second day, most delegates were fed up waiting for speakers to fiddle with their laptops, and, because word had got out about their amusing session, my two speakers found themselves with audiences of sixty or seventy instead of their allotted thirty. Result!

Preparing Yourself

Dealing with practicalities is only one aspect of preparing yourself for a presentation. Even more important is preparing yourself physically, mentally and vocally.

Choose Your Favourite Chocolate

The following exercises are proven ways to warm up your voice, relax your body, calm your mind and loosen any tension. If you do pilates or yoga or have attended antenatal classes, some of these may be familiar to you. They are all exercises that actors use on a daily basis.

I am conscious that people who work in business often don't see the value in these exercises, or at least in some of them, though I can assure you that they work and that your performance will be the better for following them. You can, if you like, treat these as chocolates in a chocolate assortment from which you can pick your favourites; use the exercises that you find work for you, but please don't ignore the others.

The Golden Thread

First, you need to be standing upright. Imagine that there is a golden thread that runs up your spine from your coccyx through each and every vertebra until it emerges from the top of your head. Stand with your feet hip-width apart and arms by your side, and consciously feel how your feet are in contact with the floor. Now, imagine a benign being somewhere above you giving a gentle, steady tug on that golden thread so you grow half an inch. At the same time, imagine a friend gently pressing down on your shoulders. This is your golden thread position and it is a very powerful one. As well as making you feel that you are 'walking tall', it undoubtedly helps to give you that indefinable quality: presence. If you want to look authoritative, remember the golden thread.

Being Present

As I have mentioned presence, it is worth adding a few more words on that crucial subject. A presentation requires you both to give the audience a present and to be present yourself. It is not by accident that these words originate from the same root. Being present means focusing all your energy on the task in hand, ignoring all extraneous thoughts. Be there for the audience, concentrate on them and on the words you are saying to them, at the moment you are saying them. For many actors, being present is the *sine qua non* of giving a good performance – unless they are wholly present, completely focused on the here and now, they will lack authenticity and their whole performance will suffer. Athletes and other top performers often talk about being 'in the zone', when they are oblivious to everything but the task at hand. They are genuinely, completely 'present'.

Stretching (and Yawning) and Feeling Grounded

Now, we need to get the blood flowing and to relax your muscles. Imagine that you are surrounded by a sea of oozing mud. Place your foot firmly into the mud and let your weight press down into it. Then bring your foot back and admire your magnificent footprint. Do this several times, first with one foot and then with the other. You may find that you can feel your feet and how they are in contact with the ground much more noticeably now. In the theatre, we often talk about the importance of feeling 'grounded', and this exercise is all about enhancing that feeling – your base should be solid and you should feel strong and in control.

Imagine that you are surrounded by a sphere of mud, and

that it's just at the edge of your reach. Push one hand into the mud, really stretch and then pull your hand out and admire your handprint. Repeat this several times, first with one hand and then with the other.

Another way to stretch your arms (and your jaw) is to yawn. Really yawn, let the sound come out, stretch your arms and open your jaw. When I do this in a course, you can often see participants trying desperately to yawn with their mouths closed in an attempt to stay 'polite' or 'elegant'. No, really open your mouth and yawn loudly – you need to get that jaw working.

Where Do You Get Tense?

Many people, when they get nervous, localise the tension in their neck and shoulders. To release the tension, it nearly always helps to scrunch your muscles even further before relaxing them. Scrunch your hands into fists, bend your elbows, bring your shoulders up to your ears and scrunch your face as tightly as you can. Then relax – face first, then shoulders, then let your arms hang loosely down and finally relax your hands and give them a shake out.

*Please note that the following exercises must be done very gently and must **never** hurt you – if they do, or if you have had neck or shoulder problems in the past, stop doing them straightaway!*

Or you could try this: Hold your head up and then look to the right and let your head follow your eyes – you should feel the muscles on the left of your neck stretching. Come back to the centre, pause, then look to the left and let your head follow your eyes, then back to the centre again. Now let your head fall slowly forward until your chin is on your chest – you should feel the muscles at the back of your neck stretching. Bring your head back upright. Now let your head slowly tilt backwards, leaving your lower jaw behind so that your mouth opens. Come back to the centre and repeat the whole exercise three or four times. If you can, try breathing in as you turn your head, and breathing out as you bring your head back to the centre.

Not everyone gets tense in their neck and shoulders. It is very effective just to tense each set of muscles one after the other, starting with scrunching your toes, then calves, thighs, buttocks, tummy, and finally chest, each time relaxing the muscles before moving onto the next set. I often find that doing this exercise will help people realise where they hold their tension so that they know which bit to concentrate on in future.

Move for a Purpose

By the way, I am a great believer in using scrunching of the toes to combat aimless wandering when presenting. Scrunch your toes and then try to walk – it's not impossible though it doesn't come easily. If you tend to do that well-known wandering barn dance as you present, scrunch your toes instead and you will find that you stop. When you are presenting, you must move for a purpose – to punctuate what you are saying, to address a new topic to a specific part of the audience or to allow a pause while your audience thinks. Aimless wandering is just distracting. Michael MacIntyre can get away with it because that highly energetic pacing up and down the stage is part of his stage persona, though I wouldn't recommend it to most speakers!

Take a Deep Breath (or Several) for Inspiration

Back to our exercises. Now we have relaxed your body a little, we need to move on to breathing. I call this exercise 'The Flower and the Candle', though it would perhaps be more accurate to call it 'Your Favourite Scent and the Candle'. Imagine that you have in front of you a wonderful example of the thing you most like to smell in the world. I suggest a flower, though it could be anything. Course participants have come up with a whole range – a bacon buttie, fresh bread, new-mown grass, petrol and even 'the smell of my baby's neck after a bath'. Bring this wonderfully scented thing up to your nose and take a deep inhalation – magic! I call this your 'inspiration' as that literally means breathing in.

From Inspiration to Expression

Now, stretch your arm out (not too far) and give a 'thumbs-up'. Through the miracle of your imagination, that thumb now becomes a lit candle. Purse your lips and blow at the candle flame, not to blow it out but to make it flicker with a steady and firm out breath, sustained at the same level throughout. This is your 'expression'. You are literally expressing the air. Ensure there is no tension in your neck during this – you do not need to force the breath by jutting the head forward.

Now repeat the inspiration and the expression several times. You should find that you are drawing the air deep down into your lungs. If you put your hand on your diaphragm (just above your belly button), you should find that the muscles expand as you breathe in and contract as you breathe out. If you ever get a chance to watch an opera singer or a synchronised swimmer do this, prepare to be astonished at the extent to which their diaphragm expands – it's called 'rib-swing'.

Breathing for Air and Relaxation

There are a couple of really important reasons why you should do this 'Flower and Candle' exercise. One is a technical reason. If you are not breathing deeply enough (a common problem if you tend to get tension in your neck and shoulders), you will not have enough air to support your voice. Your voice will become thin and squeaky or you will run out of breath, neither of which is going to give a good impression of you as a presenter. Remember, you are a wind instrument.

Second, deep breathing like this will calm you down, so you will feel less tense in the first place. The mind and the body cannot be separated. If you are panicking about making a speech, for example, your body will respond to your feelings of panic by tensing up. Equally, if your body is relaxed and comfortable, and you are breathing deeply, your brain will pick up these physical signals and you will begin to feel more relaxed generally.

What's Your 10-10-10 Moment?

Another exercise that helps many people is to imagine yourself at a time when you have been performing at your best. It is often called a 10-10-10 moment – a time when you have been ten out of ten for energy, commitment and focus. It might have been the moment when you scored **that** goal, or perhaps when you were skiing down a black run and could feel the wind in your face and the shush-shush of your skis on the snow. Or it might have been a quieter moment, perhaps when you walked down the aisle on your wedding day or when you held your baby in your arms for the first time, or when your boss said '*really well* *done'*. It doesn't matter really, it just has to be a moment when you felt fantastic, on top of the world, as though you could do anything.

The key is to paint a picture of that moment in your mind's eye as vividly as you can, with bright colours (or sharp contrasts if you think in black and white). Once you have the picture in your mind's eye, fill it out with the other senses. Were there sounds? Music or the sound of the sea or cheering perhaps. Could you feel anything? The grass under your feet or the texture of your clothes maybe. Or perhaps you could smell or taste something. Use all your senses to get to as complete a memory as you can.

Now remember how you felt at that moment, and let that positive, amazing feeling suffuse your body. That is your 10-10-10 moment. If you remember your 10-10-10 moment and how it made you feel just before you stand up to present, it will almost certainly make you look more confident and banish any nerves. It doesn't work for everyone, though it is well worth a try as in my experience, it works for most people.

Warming Up Your Voice

Now that you are standing tall and feeling confident and relaxed, let's work on the mechanics of your voice. There are many physical and vocal exercises you could do; here are a few of my favourites:

Hum and Hum Again

Choose your favourite hum. You should find your throat is open and the sound is probably resonating in the top part of your face (around your sinus area). Try to hum for at least two minutes; once you've established your favourite hum, modulate the note so that you explore your vocal range from angry great bumblebee to ambulance siren. After a bit, try to bring the sound down so it is resonating in your mouth; this should make your lips tingle too as it brings the sound forward.

Find a comfortable hum and then modulate it up and down, still with your lips tingling. Then try humming while you chew a huge piece of imaginary toffee and vary the pitch. Mmmmmmm! Hum on a specific sound – V-V-V-V like a car starting, or Z-Z-Z-Z like an angry wasp. If you know you have problems with particular sounds, change from a hum to making those sounds.

Fix your eyes on the far side of the room at a point a little above the eye line. Keep humming fairly low down in your register but 'think' your energy **up** to that point on the wall. The sense should be that your voice is flowing out in an arc towards that distant spot. Moving away from your hum, try calling *'Hi!'* and *'Hello'* across the room, first to a friend and then to someone you don't like. Note the difference. Try getting louder and softer, though always sending the sound out on that arc.

Loosen Your Lips

To get your lips working well, make horsey sounds, with your lips as loose as possible, or make the sound of a motorbike going up through the gears. Make a face like a pig's snout and then form a great big grin like the Cheshire Cat. Repeat the snout and the grin – quicker! Many people have really lazy mouths – notably the Royal Family and many cockneys – and this is a way of getting the lips moving.

And Your Tongue

Can you touch the tip of your nose with your tongue? Or your chin? Try it. Then stick your tongue out and rotate it. It's as well to do this exercise with a handkerchief at the ready!

Try Some Tongue Twisters

Now you are ready to start saying something more than

just '*Hi!*', so try some tongue twisters. The theatre world has lots of favourites:

Vivacious Vivien's voracious vehicle veritably oozed va-va-voom.

Try really rolling the 'r' in voracious and veritably, if you can.

She stood upon the balustraded balcony
Inexplicably mimicking him hiccupping
And amicably welcoming him in.

This is a real favourite of mine. There is a sort of story going on – why is she on the balcony? Is she welcoming a guest to a party? So you need to try to reflect the sense of the words in the way you say them. The second line ought to be light and springy to mirror the sense and sound of the words. And finally the last line can be expansive, perhaps with a welcoming gesture. The '*in/im*' sounds are particularly tricky to say one after the other and require lots of lip and jaw movement.

One wily woman wool-winder winds wool which wouldn't wind.

Try this with your upper lip pinched between your thumb and forefinger.

*Can you imagine an imaginary menagerie manager
imagining managing an imaginary menagerie?*

*To sit in solemn silence in a dull, dark, dock
In a pestilential prison with a life-long lock
Awaiting the sensation of a short sharp shock
From a cheap and chippy chopper on a big black block.*

You need to really emphasise all the consonants – especially at the ends of words – in this bit of Gilbert and Sullivan. Try this one with your tongue pressed against your top teeth, and then again with your tongue working freely. I often find with course participants that just doing this one exercise can completely change the quality of their articulation.

*All I want is a proper cup of coffee
Made in a proper copper coffee pot.
You can believe it or not,
But I just want a cup of coffee
In a proper coffee pot.
Tin coffee pots
Or iron coffee pots
Are of no use to me.
If I can't have
A proper cup of coffee
In a proper copper coffee pot,
I'll have a cup of tea!*

There are many more to be found on the internet, from the short *(Unique New York)* to the frankly impossible *(Freshly fried flying fish, freshly fried flesh)*. Again, note which sounds you find difficult to articulate and find tongue twisters that test you.

These Exercises Really Work

These sorts of exercises might seem to you to be a step too far, and yet I know that a few minutes work like this can make a huge difference to how a presenter looks and sounds. Most audiences may not consciously notice if you are speaking well – articulately, smoothly, with clear enunciation – though they will certainly notice if you are not. If professional performers do these warm-ups, so should you. At least, I assume you want to be seen as a professional rather than a rank amateur?

A ballerina might do an hour's warm-up before a performance, as she will be putting her body through its paces in ways that the vast majority of us cannot imagine. For most of us, a few minutes will make a huge difference. I am fully aware that most business people lead busy lives and rush from meeting to meeting and from phone call to presentation with hardly a pause in between. Yet even if you only choose to do one or two of these exercises before a speech or a meeting, your performance will improve significantly – guaranteed. I recommend nipping to the loo or going for a quick walk around the building while you get yourself prepared in whatever way is going to help you.

I said at the start of this section that this was a chocolate assortment from which to choose your favourites – tuck in!

Key Points to Remember

* Consider the audience, the venue, the possibilities of anything going wrong, and your own needs, and prepare accordingly.

* Take a few minutes to warm yourself up, physically, vocally and mentally.

* 'Eat' lots of your favourite 'chocolates'.

---

8. Dealing with the Dreaded Questions

Dealing with questions is a constant source of worry for many speakers, though there is no need to panic. Read this chapter and you will understand how to ask for them and how to answer them.

What's in this Chapter?

*   Prepare for questions in advance
*   How to invite questions
*   Waiting for questions to come
*   Asking the audience a question
*   Repeating the question so everyone can hear
*   Dealing with questions you don't want
*   Ending on a high.

You Don't Have to Invite Questions

Of course, you may well not want any questions. If that is the case, just don't invite them. Finish your speech on a high, acknowledge the applause and leave the platform/room or sit down. However, most speeches leave the possibility of questions open and it is important to recognise that the moment you invite questions from your audience, your role changes. You stop being just a presenter and become more of a facilitator, so you must now manage the interaction with the audience.

Prepare for the Questions

Like any good facilitator or presenter, you must prepare before the event. Think of the questions you might get asked and prepare the answers. Particularly, think of the questions that you **don't** want to be asked and prepare ways of answering them – there are suggestions for dealing with these later on in this chapter.

How to Ask for Questions

Many speakers let their presentations peter out in a feeble way and then tack *'Any questions?'* onto their last sentence with hardly a pause or a change of tone. Don't be one of that benighted crew.

First, remember the words of Sam Goldwyn and make sure that your presentation ends with a climax:

'So *before you leave today, I want you all to sign my petition – and you're not going home till you have.'*

139

'If we don't change the way we operate now, we won't be able to afford this conference next year.'

'Just remember, we leave this world to our children, and our children's children – and we must leave it fit for purpose.'

By the way, try not to end a presentation with *'Thank you'* – it's hardly a climax.

Second, leave the audience with your last key point ringing in their ears. Take a pause. Acknowledge the applause (if it is that kind of presentation). Look around. Smile. Enjoy your success. Then say something like:

'I suspect that some of you have found what I have said somewhat contentious (or rather technical, or a bit shocking, or whatever). I see a few nods, so perhaps there are some questions you would like to ask? Fire away.'

This is much better than just saying *'Any questions?'* It's a more interesting comment and it leads the audience to ask about the element of your presentation that you want questions on. You could be more specific still: *'I didn't really have time today to go into enormous detail about alternative ways of linking the FCG403B to the transceiver, though we have a few minutes now, so if anyone would like to ask a question around that, please do.'*

Waiting for the Questions to Come

At this point, it is not unusual for there to be dead silence. Let it hang for a good while. It can take quite a lot of courage for someone, particularly in a large audience, to ask the first question. And what seems like forever to you can be valuable thinking time for an audience. After leaving enough time, you may need to prompt them: *'Anyone? I noticed there was a sharp intake of collective breath when I suggested that our education system needs to give as much emphasis to drama and dance as to mathematics.'*

What if there are No Questions?

If there is still silence, you can choose either to say something like: *'Well, if I have stunned you into silence, let's leave it at that – but I'll be around over lunch so please don't hesitate to come and talk to me.'*

Or you could say: *'Well, I've got a question for* **you***. I suggested that we could and should be better at detecting fraud and I suggested three ways of improving our record – have any of you got any more ideas on that knotty subject?'*

And you might even end a question like the one above by adding: *'Zach, you're a specialist in fraud – what do you think?'* Zach must be someone you know and, ideally, you should have alerted him in advance that you may ask him that question. And once Zach has offered his opinion, that could open the floodgates to more questions.

I am not a great believer in planting questions – asking a mate to ask a particular question for you – as it nearly always sounds false. It is a different matter encouraging a friend to ask something to start the ball rolling if you think the audience may not otherwise ask any questions. Let the friend choose the question, though, as it will sound more natural.

Repeat the Question so it is Heard

Be aware of two other potential pitfalls in inviting questions. One relates to audibility. In almost any gathering where not everyone is sitting round a table, a question from the front may well be inaudible to those at the back. You must always repeat the question so that everyone hears what it is, and knows what you are answering. Sometimes, in a large conference, microphones are available, and you may have a better view of the person who put their hand up than the roving helpers with the mikes, so do give them clear instructions as to where to send the mikes. Don't worry about the time it takes to get the mike to the questioner – a bit of anticipation works wonders. Incidentally, even if you are wearing a mike, you need to keep your energy level up – don't assume that the mike will do the work for you. And do insist on having a proper sound check and some time to rehearse wearing the mike.

When a Question Becomes a Discussion

Second, a question may set off a debate between two members of the audience. In a small gathering that may be exactly what you wanted. In a larger conference, if you think the discussion is of less interest to the rest of the audience, you may need to cut it short and suggest that the two debaters continue their conversation outside the conference room. If the discussion is of general interest, however, and it can be heard by the rest of the audience, just efface yourself a bit and let it happen. Perching on a table works well as it shows you are interested without being involved – sitting down looks as though you have abandoned the discussion and you may feel a bit of a lemon just standing there (though you shouldn't if you show enough interest). You need to time the moment when you stand up, walk forward and take back control so you can close the matter or the session effectively.

Dealing with Interruptions

I have assumed here that you will be taking answers at the end of your presentation. In many less formal situations, you may find that people interrupt with questions as you are speaking. If you don't mind or if it is that sort of meeting, fine, answer them as best you can, or adopt one of the strategies below for answering questions to which you don't know the answer.

If you do mind, perhaps because you find interruptions cause you to lose your place or mean you get flustered, you have two choices. One is to establish early on in your speech that you want to take questions at the end; or you can say to the first questioner something like this: *'Can I deal with any questions at the end of my presentation? Please ask me again then.'* You will often find that by the end, you have answered the question in another part of your speech anyway or that the questioner will have forgotten what he or she asked. And if they do ask it again, at least you will have given yourself some time in which to consider a reply.

Sometimes, people don't so much ask a question as make a speech of their own. If you are at a formal conference, it is really the job of the conference host to interrupt if it is going on too long, though you cannot rely on that. Don't forget that standing on the platform gives you a certain authority, so you are quite within your rights to interrupt and ask if there is a question coming, though you have to be careful not to sound too rude (unless you want to, of course). More effective is to sum up briefly what the interrupter has said and ask their question for them: *'So, as I understand it, you are saying that government funding for the arts is pitifully low and you want to know what I am going to do about it. Well, I agree it is too low though I think it is the Arts Council's job, not mine, to lobby for more funding.'*

Tactics for Dealing with the Unwanted Question

First, don't rush. Plant your feet, feel grounded. Try hard not to take a step backwards – that can appear as though you want to run away. Take a deep breath – inspire yourself. In a large conference, you must repeat the question so that everyone has heard it, and even ask the questioner if you have got it right. By the way, don't have a conversation only with the person who asked the question; look at everyone and include them in the discussion.

All of this buys you time, and it may be enough time to find the answer popping into your head. It often is. If so, no problem, just answer the question. If not, there are a number of different approaches.

The Direct Riposte

If you think someone who will be at the event has an axe to grind or wants to put you on the spot, you can be pretty sure that he or she will want to ask that killer question, so make sure you have your riposte or rebuttal ready: *'Aha, I had a feeling you would ask that question, Gus. As I said to you two weeks ago, the answer is blowin' in the wind (or in your department's hands, or clearly outlined in our business plan, or whatever).'* If you can refer to an earlier discussion about this issue in your reply, as I have done above, the rest of the audience will quickly realise that Gus is just bringing it up again to score points. Fifteen-love to you.

The Honest Injun

'That's a really good question and I don't know the answer.' Unless you have been asked to present as the expert on this subject, there is no harm in saying you don't know and it can be a very powerful comment to make, if said in the right tone. You may want to add *'I can go away and look into it and if you give me your details, I'll get back to you.'* (If you say this, make sure you do!) You may also want to combine it with the next approach.

The Judo Player

*'What do **you** think?'*

Or *'We've got a room full of experts here – what does anyone think?'*

The Road Sweeper

'I think that's a rather complicated issue and we don't really have time to do it justice now – can we meet later and talk it through one-to-one?' This is particularly effective if you know the questioner has a particular axe to grind.

The Flatterer

'That's a really good question and I am not surprised, Josie, that someone of your experience should pinpoint one of the key parts of my presentation that I didn't cover in depth.' You probably now need to turn it round (see *The Judo Player* above) and ask Josie what she thinks. This approach can easily backfire, so use it with great caution. It is often combined with the next tactic.

The Political Animal

Politicians are taught not to answer a question they don't want but to answer another (vaguely) related one to which they do have an answer. This is so widely recognised now that it nearly always backfires, and you may well find that the original questioner asks his question again – and this time you probably have to try to answer it, or be forever viewed as an empty vessel. If you doubt this, google Jeremy Paxman asking Michael Howard the same question a dozen or so times and watch the video. Related (and equally risky) is the next method.

The Patroniser

'That's a very good question but I would like to widen that out and comment on. . . .' Like the Political Animal above, this allows you to answer a different question altogether – though this approach is really not recommended!

Dealing with a Persistent or Stroppy Questioner May Need a Direct Approach

'Thank you, but I think it is time to hear from other people as well.'

End on a High

Don't forget that as the presenter, you are in a position of great power and however the questions have gone, make sure you end the session by repeating your key message once more: *'Thank you for all those excellent questions – this has been a most interesting session. We have run out of time now so I just want to leave you with my key point: The competition is getting stronger and the economy is getting weaker yet we have the systems and the capacity and the desire to shape our own future – and shape it we will.'*

Don't forget too that if you have followed the advice in this book and thought about what your audience needs and wants to know and have made that the basis of your presentation, you probably answered all their questions in your speech.

A final word – enjoy the questions. Generally speaking, the audience will not be against you and will genuinely want to know what it is you have to say. If they have questions at the end, it means that your audience was stimulated by what you said and wants to know more. And that may well mean that you made a great presentation.

Key Points to Remember

* Prepare for questions in advance.

* Make sure you manage the process of interaction with your audience effectively.

* Enjoy the questions – they probably mean your audience was engaged.

---

9. An Example of a Great Speech

A great speech, one that highlights many of the techniques and rhetorical devices that I have been exploring in this book, was given by Dr Clare Gerada, then Chair of the Royal College of General Practitioners (RCGP), at the 2011 RCGP Annual Conference in Liverpool. Here is a long extract from that speech [missing passages are indicated by (...)]. I have added notes alongside the speech that refer back to the advice in this book.

I have not heard Dr Gerada give this presentation so I have no idea whether or not she is a great speaker, though I certainly know that she, and my friends Martin Shovel and Martha Leyton of CreativityWorks who worked on the presentation with her, wrote a great speech. Would that all speeches were as entertaining, relevant and powerful.

I'd like to tell you a story about a GP, a radiologist, a pathologist and a psychiatrist.	Great start
Sounds like the first line of a joke, but it isn't. The GP was me.	Make it personal

We were having dinner with our children at an open-air opera in Germany. The place was packed. Everyone was having a good time, when the dreaded happened. Out of the corner of my eye, I saw an elderly man fall headfirst into his plate.

Telling a story

The four of us looked at each other. We knew our meal was over and we swung into action. Each working to type. The psychiatrist tending to the man's wife. The radiologist searching for a defibrillator. The pathologist pounding on the poor man's chest. Me giving mouth-to-mouth.

Painting a picture

Short sentences

From the way he keeled over, it was obvious he was dead. But we knew there was still plenty for us to do. We had to comfort his distressed wife. And we had to keep the crowd calm for thirty minutes, till the paramedics arrived.

'Keeled over' – good phrase

When it was over, my fifteen-year-old son turned to me and said: 'I want to be able to do that.'

'Do what?' I asked him.

'Care for people,' he said.

Great punch-line

His reply surprised me. Not just because impressing teenage children isn't easy. But because what impressed him wasn't the glory and the drama of our public display of medical skill. No. What impressed him was our simple act of caring.

Good contrast

Caring for a sick man. Caring for the man's wife. And caring for the people in the crowd.

Rule of Three

That's what inspired my son.

And that's how my father inspired me a generation ago. It wouldn't be allowed now, but he used to take me with him on home visits in the post-war slums of Peterborough. I watched him treat children with measles and care for the dying in their homes. That's when I knew I wanted to be a doctor.

Personal experience

Why did I tell you that story? Because I believe each of us has a story about what inspired us to become a doctor. A story that made us what we are today. A story that lights our way to the future.

Rule of Three and repetition

Our stories have never been more important. Especially now, when our profession is under pressure to replace the language of caring with the language of the market. We need to remind ourselves why we entered this honourable profession in the first place.

Use of a contrast

When I come home from work and my son asks me what sort of day I've had, on a good day I want to be able to say 'I saved a life', not 'I met a budget'.

Another great contrast

Of course, it's important that GPs are mindful of resources. We have a responsibility to spend the public's money carefully and wisely. That goes without saying.

But we must never lose sight of the patient as a person, at the heart of our practice.

Patients are not 'commodities' to be bought and sold in the health marketplace.

(...)

We are already embracing the language of the market when we talk about, for example, care pathways, case management, demand management, productivity, clinical and financial alignment, risk stratification.

'Embracing' – so much more powerful than 'using'

We're already accused of making 'inappropriate referrals' whenever we put what's best for our patients above what's best for saving money.

More contrasts

(...)

I worry we're heading towards a situation where healthcare will be like a budget airline. There'll be two queues: one queue for those who can afford to pay, and another for those who can't. Seats will be limited to those who muscle in first. And the rest will be left stranded on the tarmac.

Good simile

'Muscle in' – strong verb

(...)

So what about GP commissioning? Will it help us reduce health inequalities? And will it enable us to deliver better care to our patients?

Good rhetorical questions

People often tell me that GPs make good commissioners because of the population-focus we bring to care. After all, as a profession we see 300 million patients per year. If anyone can be said to have their finger on the pulse of the nation, surely it's us.

Clever twist on a metaphor

It's an argument I've supported for decades. But we must tread carefully in this brave new world and do everything in our power to make sure it's the public's pulse we have our fingers on – not the public's purse.

Another great contrast and a play on words

Which is why I believe that big decisions – decisions like whether to close hospitals – should be the responsibility of governments, not GPs. It's the government's job to decide how much we invest in healthcare and what services the NHS should provide.

(...)

I've always said that good commissioning is about being a good GP. It's about understanding how we use resources fairly and effectively. But whatever happens we must make sure that the commissioning agenda isn't allowed to compromise our relationship with the patient in front of us. We must not risk long-term benefits being sacrificed in favour of short-term savings.

Yet another good contrast

(...)

How long will it be before we find ourselves injecting a patient's knee joint – at Injections-R-us plc – instead of referring to an orthopaedic surgeon for a knee replacement?

Nice use of ridicule

And, once referred for hospital treatment, patients must be able to trust their doctors to base care on need and not on making money for the hospital.

More contrast

(...)

Can the market achieve similar outcomes? There is plenty of evidence that market-driven health services lead to limited choice, escalating costs, reduced quality. And let's remind ourselves, the biggest health market in the world, the US, has achieved the remarkable double whammy of having the most expensive system in the world and the greatest health inequalities. It comes near the bottom of the league for most health outcomes – and boasts an unnecessary death every twelve minutes.

Rule of Three

Interesting facts

So what can we do? It would be easy to feel discouraged. But I know we all want the best for our patients, we always have and we always will. And as long as we do what we know to be right for patients, we will keep their trust.

'We' – she and her audience are in this together

We all became doctors because we wanted to make a positive difference to people's lives. It would be hard to devise a better and more inspiring way of achieving this than through the provision of excellent general practice care, within a universal health service.

In times of austerity, we need to come together so that we can collaborate, co-operate and innovate – not compete against each other.

Rule of Three **and** a contrast

You expected me to talk about the health bill in England, but this bill, like other reorganisations across the whole of the UK, will come and go. Instead I have chosen to talk to you about what matters to our patients, now and forever – a doctor who cares.

Her objective, not her topic

(...)

My message to you is simple and clear. My son wanted to practice medicine because of what he saw me and my friends do: care. If we want to keep serving the best interests of our patients, we must reject the language of the market and embrace the language of caring. And keep telling our stories.

Referring back to the start of the speech.

10. Nothing to Fear

While I was writing this book, I would occasionally mention its subject in conversations with relatives and friends. Time and again, their reaction was: *'I am terrified of public speaking – I'd rather be thrown to the lions'*. Even one or two of my colleagues who act for a living confessed that standing up to make a speech filled them with dread, even though they would be perfectly comfortable performing in a play on stage.

Public Speaking Versus Dying – No Contest

Apparently, this fear of public speaking – 'glossophobia' – is very common. In fact, most people are more afraid of making a presentation than they are of dying. It's not just that people are afraid of speaking at a conference to three hundred people, they can be equally fearful of giving a best man's speech or standing up to report on progress to a team of workmates.

On one hand, I sympathise with those people who are terrified. If you were to tell me *'Tim, today, you're going to bungee jump*', I would be quaking in my shoes in an instant. I get vertigo standing on a chair, so the idea of jumping off a high cliff with nothing but an elastic band round my ankle would really petrify me. In fact, I am getting into a cold sweat just writing about it.

So I know what it is to be terrified of something that hasn't yet happened.

What Are People Scared of?

However, there is a difference, at least in my mind. Bungee jumping is not an everyday activity (unless, of course, you run 'Bungee Jumps R Us') and, whatever they may say, there is a real element of physical danger inherent in it.

Standing up and speaking risks no such physical danger. I suppose you might trip over as you mount the stairs to the stage, or even fall off the stage. But both those disasters are pretty unlikely, and even if they did happen, there is probably going to be more damage to your pride than to your body.

Everyday Activities

What's more, standing up and speaking are both activities that you almost certainly indulge in all day, every day. You stand up to get out of bed, to walk downstairs, to make a cup of tea. If you work in an office, however sedentary your job, you will stand up to go to a meeting, to visit the toilet and to go home again.

All the time, you will be speaking. You will speak to your partner, if you have one (and if you are on speaking terms). You will speak to your colleagues at work, to the person in the station ticket booth, and you'll probably say '*Sorry!*' to the idiot who bumps into you as you try to get off at your station.

So both standing and speaking are commonplace activities, in which you already have plenty of experience and, probably, a considerable degree of expertise. When you are asked to make a speech, it is not as though someone is asking you to demonstrate your skills at, say, judo when you have never learnt judo in your life. They are asking you to do something that you do all day, every day – just to do it a bit more formally, or to more people, or with more preparation.

An Irrational Fear

So, any fear of public speaking that you may have, like my vertigo, is completely irrational. It probably stems from a desire not to look a fool when you get it 'wrong', from having hundreds of pairs of eyes bore in on you as you stand, naked and exposed, on a platform, having your every utterance analysed as though you were auditioning for 'The X Factor'.

Laugh at Your Fear

It doesn't have to be like that.

This book has been written to arm you with so many ideas, tips and techniques that you will be able to laugh at your fear. If you follow the advice in this book, you stand a very good chance of making memorable presentations that really have an impact.

Having to Make Presentations is Commonplace

That is just as well, particularly in the world of business, as it is rare that you can go through professional life without having to make a presentation at least once. I often find myself coaching people who have just been promoted, and the key thing for them that distinguishes their more senior role from their previous one is the need to give presentations. Even business people who have managed to carve out a backroom niche for themselves can suddenly get asked to present to the board about their work, and if you have ambitions to be any kind of manager, it is extremely likely that you will have to make speeches, and probably quite regularly.

You could do what most people do and stick with the old, boring, PowerPoint-dominated approach. Despite the fact that they have no positive impact whatsoever, some conferences will still consist of a succession of stultifying speeches, often accompanied by illegible and incomprehensible slides, which are pretty well guaranteed to send you to sleep or at least into a state of torpor – now universally known as 'Death by PowerPoint'.

Presentations don't have to be dull. You don't have to be dull. Even the driest subject can be made interesting by a speaker who has taken steps to engage his or her audience. And it is the interesting presentation that wins new business. It is the gripping speaker whose professional reputation is enhanced, just as it is the dull speaker who is marked down as a failure.

Enhance Your Reputation

It is really important to grasp this last point. When I started training business people, one of the first people to commission a course from me was the HR Director of a major company. He told me this story:

'The Board recently held a meeting to which two members of staff were invited to give presentations on trial projects

they were leading. Both of them were very experienced and technically highly competent, and both of them had impressive reputations.

'The first man arrived and launched confidently into his presentation. He had clearly prepared, but what stood out was the energy and passion with which he spoke. He obviously believed in his project and he knew everything there was to know about it, because whenever he was asked a question, he answered it clearly and articulately. At the end, he drove home his key point, which was that the Board should get behind his scheme and roll it out to the rest of the company.

'The second man, too, had clearly prepared, as he had written out his complete presentation on sheets of A4 which shook uncontrollably as he spoke. He had prepared some PowerPoint slides too, all of which were incomprehensible or illegible or both. He spoke to the screen or into his notes rather than to us, and so he was difficult to hear. And whenever he was asked a question, he stammered, lost his place and looked confused.

'Inevitably, the second man's career has come to a grinding halt. He is just as technically competent as his colleague but he is now seen as a joke, and his chances of promotion are zero. The first man, on the contrary, is now marked down for great things. And, not surprisingly, the Board decided to allocate funds to the first man's project and not to the other one.

'And all because he couldn't make a competent presentation.'

An Essential and Learnable Skill

That is the crunch. Being able to make a good presentation is increasingly seen as an essential skill, even a career-defining one. Like any skill, just about anyone can learn how to make a presentation to a reasonable standard, however scared they are of it. Don't forget, when you were first given a bike to ride, you were probably very wobbly and apprehensive at first. But you almost certainly cracked it in no time. You may never reach the dizzy heights of a Chris Hoy or a Victoria Pendleton, yet you can probably ride a bike competently. Or drive a car. Or draft a report. Or work out a budget. All skills you had to learn first, before you could reach a satisfactory level.

I know the advice in this book can help you give powerful, memorable and compelling presentations. I know, because I have been using these techniques with hundreds of people like you for twenty-five years. And I have seen the most tongue-tied, most shambolic, most boring speakers come alive and speak with confidence and impact after working with them for a day or two, even sometimes for just half an hour. If you act on the advice in this book, so could you.

I would also appeal to you that you learn by studying other great speeches. You can deduce from that that I mean great speeches other than your own, because I am confident that you will now be able to deliver compelling, powerful presentations yourself.

Give and Get Good, Honest Feedback

Nevertheless, as the philosopher, George Santayana, once said: '*The wisest mind has something yet to learn.*' However well you think you have delivered a presentation and however many congratulations you receive, you could probably have done something even better.

So, be critical of yourself. Seek genuine and honest feedback from people you know and trust. If you have a big speech coming up, bring in a good presentation skills coach or an experienced actor and benefit from their pearls of wisdom.

Reach for the Stars

And aim high. Don't just aspire to be the best speaker in your department or your organisation. Set your sights on being viewed as one of the great speakers of your profession, or even more.

Follow the advice in this book and you can do it.

Summary

To sum up, the core advice on how to make presentations that wow your audience is:

* **Aim for more energy**. Almost all the executives I work with benefit from attacking their speeches with more energy. It makes their voice more interesting, they find that their body starts to come alive and what they are saying comes across with more passion and conviction.

* **You must connect** with your audience. Make sure you look them in the eye and focus on them. It's never just about information. Think about how you want your audience to feel.

* **Don't use PowerPoint** – please! You may think it helps but it almost certainly doesn't help the audience and there are so many other, more creative ways of getting your points across.

* If you really have to use PowerPoint, **use pictures more than words**.

* If PowerPoint is just an aid to you **rather than a benefit to the audience**, you shouldn't be using it. Write yourself some notes instead.

* **Use my Post-it note process** to create contents and a structure to your presentation. Take your audience on a journey.

* **Make sure you have an objective** as well as a topic. Your objective is probably to sell something – an idea, a product, yourself.

* Remember **you are giving your audience a 'present'**, so give them one they want or need.

* Remember Sam Goldwyn. **Start with an earthquake and build to a climax!**

* Give your presentations **a touch of creativity**. Tell them stories, or find a powerful metaphor.

* **Use props or interact with your audience.** A presentation does not have to be just a speaker on a stage, spouting away.

* Be mindful of how you can make your presentations **different, imaginative and memorable**.

* Think about the language you are using. **Use simple, jargon-free English.**

* **Spice up your speech** with a sprinkling of more unusual words or phrases.

* **Use rhetorical devices** like anaphora and the Rule of Three – they work.

* **Rehearse thoroughly**. If you haven't rehearsed, you are not ready to deliver.

* **Rehearse by 'putting it on its feet'**. You cannot rehearse in your head.

* **Get feedback** from a friend, partner or colleague so you know how you are coming across.

* **Prepare.** Think about the audience, the room set-up, and other practical issues. Anticipate problems.

* **Warm yourself up**, physically, vocally, and mentally. Warm-up exercises really do help.

* **Prepare for questions** in advance.

* **Manage the question-and-answer process** carefully. It is not the same as giving a presentation.

* **Relish the questions** you get as it means your audience was engaged.

* **Learn by studying other great speeches**.

Follow this advice and you will have equipped yourself with all the tools you need, so get out there and wow your audiences!

Bibliography

There are many other books on the market that touch on some of the material that I have covered in this book. These are just a few of my favourites:

The Salmon of Knowledge: Stories for Work, Life, the Dark Shadow, and Oneself, Nick Owen, Crown House Publishing, Camarthen. Nick Owen has published a number of good books on stories.

How to Get Ideas, Jack Foster, Berrett-Koehler Publishers. This is a very readable and straightforward book on developing your creativity.

Language Intelligence: Lessons on Persuasion from Jesus, Shakespeare, Lincoln and Lady Gaga, Joseph J. Romm. This book explores rhetorical devices in more detail than I have.

Advanced Banter: The QI Book of Quotations, John Lloyd and John Mitchenson, Faber and Faber. Absolutely the best book of quotations I have come across.

Lost for Words: The Mangling and Manipulation of the English Language, John Humphrys, Hodder and

Stoughton. The experienced journalist and broadcaster on saying things clearly.

The Need for Words: Voice and the Text, Patsy Rodenburg, Methuen Drama. This book might be too technical for some, but Patsy Rodenburg is **the** guru of vocal brilliance, and she has some good advice on making speeches.